MW01506387

PASS

MAINSTREAM

Inclusion for Students with Behavior Disorders

Positive

Approach to

Student

Success

James R.
POOLE

Hope
CAPERTON-
BROWN

Published in the United States by
Pacific Northwest Publishing
2451 Willamette St.
Eugene, Oregon 97405
www.pacificnwpublish.com

10 9 8 7 6   5 4 3 2

ISBN: 978-1-59909-031-3

Cover design: Hannah Bontrager
Interior design: Natalie Conaway
Graphics provided by Clipart.com, © 2009 Jupiterimages Corporation, and Fotolia.com.

Pacific
Northwest
Publishing

Eugene, Oregon | www.pacificnwpublish.com

TABLE OF CONTENTS

James R. Poole, B.A. & Hope Caperton Brown, Ed.D.

JAMES POOLE is a specialist on behavior disorders and discipline and is the designer of the PASS program. He developed PASS in 1992 to provide an alternative to segregated levels-system approaches to the education of students with behavior disorders. The Houston ISD acknowledged his accomplishments in educating difficult children with the *Special Education Teacher of the Year* award in 1993. James also received appointments as faculty advisor to Teach for America in 1993–1996 and as lead behavior specialist in Galena Park ISD. As a result of the success of the PASS program, James has been asked to present the PASS approach at area and state conferences on positive approaches to managing the behavior of children with emotional and behavioral disorders. James is married to Dr. Hope Caperton-Brown. They share a passion for positive approaches to behavior management, scuba diving, and their grandchild, Elizabeth.

DR. HOPE CAPERTON-BROWN, co-developer of the PASS Program, is a licensed psychologist and licensed specialist in school psychology. She has more than 30 years of educational experience as a classroom teacher, school counselor, director of psychological services, psychologist in private practice, and university professor. Dr. Caperton-Brown has presented at national, regional, and local conferences on topics such as positive approaches to behavior management in school settings, the impact of drug/alcohol dependence, neuropsychology in schools, gender identity, effective parenting, anxiety disorders in school-age children, and special education discipline. Her research includes publications on the relationship between drug and alcohol dependence and cooperative behavior. For the last five years, Dr. Caperton-Brown has consulted with and trained schools on the PASS process. Dr. Caperton-Brown was selected as the recipient of the *2002 Outstanding School Psychologist Award* presented by the Texas Association of School Psychologists.

The authors offer PASS training through Safe & Civil Schools (800/323-8819, www.safeandcivilschools.com).

ACKNOWLEDGMENTS

Many individuals have supported the development of the PASS program. We wish to thank them for their encouragement, assistance, and friendship.

Jean Rothenberg, Licensed Specialist in School Psychology, who introduced Hope and Jim and thus enabled the creation of PASS.

Maryland Hendrix, Assistant Superintendent for Curriculum and Instruction, Galena Park ISD, who saw the potential of PASS and allowed us to develop a districtwide system of support for students with behavioral and emotional disorders.

Milton Villacorta, PASS paraprofessional, who was working with Jim and supporting the process from the very beginning.

Peter Moore, Ph.D., PASS consultant, who has made the PASS journey with us and has brought the word about PASS to many of the schools implementing this system.

The following PASS specialists and school administrators, who helped us formulate and refine PASS practices:

*   *Rhondy Long, Behavior Specialist, Galena Park ISD*
*   *Vincent Thomas, Former PASS Consultant*
*   *Mary Stewart, Former PASS Specialist*
*   *Rene Martin & Cathy Bowen, Lead Behavior Specialists, Galena Park ISD*
*   *Kresha Lane, Supervisor of Behavior Training Center, Galena Park ISD*
*   *Patricia Reynolds & Cindy Brown, Katy ISD Lead Behavior Specialists*
*   *Carolyn Meeks, Special Education Director, Lamar Consolidated ISD*
*   *Jewlon Morris, Behavior/Autism Program Supervisor, Lamar Consolidated ISD*
*   *Matt Zentell, Supervisor of Special Education, Burleson ISD*
*   *Karen King, Behavior Consultant, University of Kentucky Special Education Cooperative*

We would also like to offer our thanks to Marilyn Sprick and K Daniels of Pacific Northwest Publishing for their support in the development of this manual. Their professionalism, expertise, and warm encouragement was beyond value to us.

Finally, to our family we offer our heartfelt appreciation for their support of us as we launched PASS from a district program to one implemented nationally. Thank you LaVerne, Taul, Christine, and Lynn. And for your active, and frequently unpaid, help, we particularly want to thank Gail, Tami, Elizabeth, and Christopher. You guys are the best!

TESTIMONIALS

"PASS is everything we were looking for in a program for students with behavioral challenges. It is a proactive approach that focuses on keeping students in mainstream classes with monitoring and support. The PASS staff not only work on the re-teaching of appropriate behaviors with students but provide support and resources for the teachers as well.

"Administrators and teachers are amazed at the difference! Referrals are down and there are fewer class disruptions. Our students have had much success with PASS. They are more accountable and responsible for their behavior, and in turn they are more prepared.

"PASS is an excellent program!"

Trish Reynolds, Behavior Specialist
Katy ISD
Katy, Texas

"The PASS Program is the best thing that has ever happened for students with behavior challenges and disorders as far as I am concerned! Having taught this population in a self-contained classroom for several years, I can tell you that the PASS program has saved lives and drastically changed others for the better. It has also served to facilitate the Positive Behavior Support efforts on campuses and in districts where it is implemented. I will never work in a district without it!"

Cathy Bowen, District Behavior Specialist
Galena Park ISD
Houston, Texas

"I was ready to quit teaching, then PASS came along. Now I love my job!"

Anthony Arnold, PASS Specialist
Dunbar High School
Lexington, Kentucky

"PASS: Hard work, but the payoff is completely worth it!"

Crystal Ware, Fannie Bush Elementary
Clark County Schools
Winchester, Kentucky

"Central Kentucky Special Education Cooperative began implementing PASS in 2007 to address a high number of out-of-school suspensions for our most challenging students. PASS has been implemented in 17 of our schools: four elementary schools, five middle schools, seven high schools, and one alternative school. These schools come from different regions with diverse populations—they range from small, low-income schools to very large, prominent schools. We have one school district, Fayette County, that has implemented the PASS program in all of its high schools for the past two years, with remarkable results. In addition, Madison County School District in Richmond, Kentucky, chose to implement the PASS program for all of its high schools and middle schools in conjunction with restructuring its middle schools, high schools, and alternative school for the 2008-2009 year. All districts combine the PASS program with social skills curriculum programs from Dr. Randy Sprick, Tom Jackson, and Christian Moore. The structure of PASS is combined with the research-based social skills programs CHAMPs: Discipline in the Secondary Classroom, Why Try?, *and* Social Skills that Teach. *The results: All schools have shown a dramatic reduction in both in-school and out-of-school suspensions, office referrals, and increased attendance with the students who participated in the program."*

Combined statement from:
Karen King, Behavior Consultant
Central Kentucky Special Education Cooperative, Lexington, Kentucky

Dr. Karen Frohoff, Special Education Director
Madison County Schools, Richmond, Kentucky

"ROTC is a great leadership program and I really like it. In fact, I think I might join the military when I graduate. I miss the PASS program a very great deal. I'm serious when I say that. I wish I could be an eighth grader again so that I could come back to the junior high."

**Student who participated in PASS, then
moved to a school without a PASS program**
Statement provided by Trish Reynolds, Katy ISD, Katy, Texas

"PASS has been the most successful program that we have implemented in Galena Park for students with emotional/behavioral disabilities. PASS, from the very beginning of its implementation in 1998 as a pilot program on one campus, began to positively impact the behavior of students who were previously in self-contained classes where it was difficult to exit. They were able to remain in their regular classes with behavior specialist support for both the students and teachers. We hoped to expand to other campuses over time, and the result was that all of our principals wanted to move to the PASS program. Our students continue to benefit educationally and socially by being with their peers. Over time their self-discipline and social skills significantly improve, which results in improved rates of success on state assessments, passing grades, and improved graduation rates."

**Maryland Lee Hendrix, Associate Superintendent
of Curriculum and Instruction**
Galena Park ISD
Houston, Texas

"If, as a Director of Special Education, you are intent on seeing that your kids have the most access to the general education curriculum possible while they develop the skills to be able to assimilate themselves into the 'real world,' then PASS is the answer. Since we brought the PASS program to Lamar CISD, our behavioral kids have never done better! The introduction of the program was somewhat rocky. Our kids had been self-contained so long that they didn't know there was an outside world! There was even some fear and resentment that these kids would cause problems on 'the outside.' Imagine everyone's surprise when PASS made everything better for all children. Infractions are down, attendance is up, and test scores have gone up. What more could a district ask for? And how better could we serve our kids? Come and visit us. Many have, and now they too are using PASS!"

Carolyn Meeks, Special Education Director
Lamar Consolidated ISD, Richmond, Texas

CHAPTER 1

WHAT IS THE PASS PROGRAM?

Eddie is in kindergarten. He is explosive and occasionally violent. He cries in response to academic frustration, particularly with reading assignments. He hits his teacher and other staff members. When he is discouraged, Eddie's response is to run. He runs from his classroom, the cafeteria, and his physical education class. Eddie's classroom teacher grows increasingly frustrated and hopeless. She wants him out of her classroom.

Eventually, Eddie is assessed by the special education team, who identify him as Emotionally Disturbed. They recommend that Eddie be placed in a self-contained behavior program.

PASS (Positive Approach to Student Success) came to be because of students like Eddie. Founded on the belief that children and youth benefit both behaviorally from educational experiences with their nonhandicapped peers and academically from participation in the general curriculum, PASS provides educational services within mainstream settings to students with behavioral issues.

PASS serves both general education students whose behavior problems have identified them as at-risk and students who have been identified by special education as Emotionally/Behaviorally Disordered (EBD).

PASS is a comprehensive, multilevel program that incorporates practices consistent with IDEA Amendments (1997 and 2004) and No Child Left Behind (NCLB, 2001). The program incorporates:

- Positive Behavior Supports (PBS)

- Scientifically based research practices and interventions

- Student placement in mainstream settings where there is access to the general curriculum and highly qualified teachers

PASS involves four phases of implementation:

- Preplacement

- Orientation

- Inclusion and Maintenance

- Aftercare

Students progress through the phases, beginning with a brief period of self-contained instruction in pro-social replacement behaviors and advancing to full inclusion with individually determined levels of monitoring and support from the PASS specialist. The length of time any student remains in each phase is determined by student progress as he or she participates in PASS activities.

PASS is also about providing students with enhanced access to academic instruction from subject-area and grade-level teachers.

With the ongoing support of a PASS specialist, each student in PASS learns, practices, and implements individualized strategies that address targeted behaviors of concern. By combining targeted and intensive social skills instruction with behavior monitoring and coaching, PASS facilitates the student's development of self-management skills. Students in PASS benefit from social learning opportunities with all peers, increased access to the general curriculum, and individualized behavior support.

Throughout the program, students may also be supported by counseling (as a related service) and ongoing consultation between the PASS specialist, campus administrator, school psychologist, school counselor, mainstream teachers, and parents. PASS students are frequently monitored, and the resulting data is used in making instructional decisions. PASS students also participate in a reward system to increase student buy-in.

At its core, PASS is about educating—providing both instruction and practice in the social skills that students need to be successful in life.

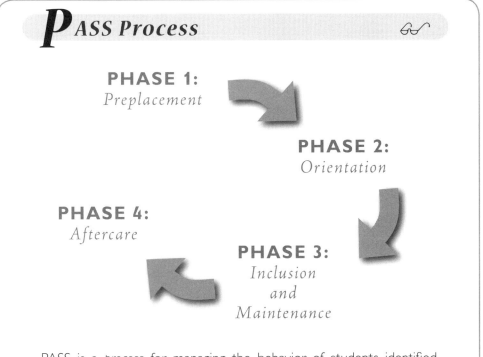

PASS Process

PHASE 1:
Preplacement

PHASE 2:
Orientation

PHASE 4:
Aftercare

PHASE 3:
*Inclusion
and
Maintenance*

PASS is a *process* for managing the behavior of students identified as behaviorally at-risk or emotionally/behaviorally disturbed. PASS incorporates a nonlevels-based, individualized approach that provides explicit teaching of behavioral expectations in mainstream settings. The program uses a Functional Behavior methodology with daily and weekly behavioral analysis to guide intervention.

PASS is also about providing students with enhanced access to academic instruction from subject-area and grade-level teachers. The primary role of the PASS specialist is to assist students in constructing appropriate replacement behaviors for the maladaptive behavior(s) that interfere with their education. The program is not about better ways to punish inappropriate behavior but about positive ways to achieve success.

The PASS approach to education is inclusive. After a brief period of time within the PASS classroom, students move to mainstream educational settings. It is our belief that academic placements in which the student has interactions with appropriate peer models and behavioral training that occurs within the natural environment at the point of performance are powerful agents of behavior change.

PASS is not a panacea that produces effective behavior change for all students. Instead, it is part of a continuum of services, ranging from the less restrictive or intensive to those that are more so. Students in a prolonged period of behavioral crisis or those with behaviors that pose a serious risk of harm to themselves or others may not be appropriate for PASS services. However, most school districts that implement PASS find that the majority of their students identified as EBD are effectively served by PASS instruction.

Schools that have adopted the PASS approach to educating students with behavioral and/or emotional issues have observed:

- Students who participate in PASS show an increase in self-esteem.

- Fewer students are placed in out-of-district placements or self-contained programs.

- Personnel who facilitate the PASS program use proactive, rather than reactive, interventions.

- PASS students have increased access to the general curriculum.

- Students identified with EBD receive more individualized behavior support.

Whence PASS?   *Reflections by Jim Poole*

The inspiration for the PASS process began in a Texas self-contained special education classroom populated by students identified as Seriously Emotionally Disturbed. These students had special transportation to and from school, arriving and leaving 30 minutes earlier than the mainstream population. A special education teacher provided all academic instruction within the self-contained classroom. Some mainstream classes were a part of the students' day—physical education, art, and music—but students were accompanied to these classes by staff. The teacher used the traditional five-level approach to classroom management, wherein all students worked for the same reinforcers and experienced the same consequences for misbehavior.

I was the teacher for this group, and over time I grew to feel that my students were the most misunderstood and poorly educated on campus. The segregation of these students and special arrangements for their school attendance led to a perception on the part of adult staff that these children were "bad" kids, dangerous, and best educated away from their peers. Some campus teachers called this group "the throwaway kids" and felt that they were just a few years away from imprisonment. One teacher went so far as to ask, "Why do we issue student numbers to these kids? It would be more efficient to just issue prison numbers."

Across the hall from my classroom was a kindergarten class. On a daily basis, the teacher would call me in to help her deal with one particular student—Eddie. Eventually, Eddie was assessed by the special education team and found to demonstrate characteristics of an Intermittent Explosive Disorder. They identified him as Emotionally Disturbed and placed him in my self-contained behavior program.

Working with Eddie, I came to believe that his frustration, and the behaviors that grew out of that frustration, stemmed from deficits in social areas. At lunch, Eddie would eat with his hands and take food off other students' trays. He simply didn't know how to ask for assistance. He didn't know how to interact positively with his fellow students or how to meet the school's behavioral expectations for the cafeteria and hallway.

Within the self-contained setting, I began to teach Eddie the social skills he was missing. He showed some progress on these new skills, and I noticed a reduction in outbursts, down from daily occurrences to a few times a week. Eddie even developed a positive relationship with adult staff in our classroom, but these positive interactions didn't generalize outside of the room. It became apparent to me that Eddie would not be able to internalize his new skills unless he was given the opportunity to practice them in the mainstream. However, the rigid structure of the levels system made this virtually impossible.

In fact, I felt that *all* of my students would benefit from a behavior program with more flexibility, where Eddie and others in my program could be taught the social skills they lacked and then move quickly into the natural setting for practice with those behaviors. Consequently, I started to look for existing programs that offered this flexibility. Despite my best efforts, all of the published programs I found displayed characteristics of the self-contained levels approach that I was already using.

So I turned to my colleagues. In calls to behavior education teachers with whom I'd worked, I learned that many felt as I did about students with behavior issues—that our students lacked information regarding what good behavior looked like and that more time should be spent on teaching social skills. From these experienced mentors, I gleaned valuable information about effective practices outside the levels system.

Armed with this information, I established a goal—to create a behavior management system that emphasized behavior education *and* provided opportunities for students to practice replacement behaviors in natural settings where they had access to positive peer models. The resulting program would become PASS.

I felt that all of my students would benefit from a behavior program with more flexibility.

All of this occurred in 1994. In 1997, Dr. Hope Caperton-Brown joined me in the ongoing development and refinement of PASS. Recognizing the opportunities PASS created for students with behavioral disorders, Hope began disseminating the PASS process to colleagues. At the same time, she began developing many of the behavior education components of PASS. The current strategies related to re-direction, FBA (Functional Behavior Assessment) approach to data analysis, and Aftercare are Hope's contributions. Many resources that make it possible for other professionals to replicate PASS have been jointly created by both Hope and me, but with Hope's vision, organization, and knowledge of research findings, PASS went from the classroom to the district level. Today, PASS is the primary approach to educating students with emotional or behavioral problems in more than 20 Texas school districts and 12 schools in Kentucky.

Case Study

The year after I met Eddie, I implemented PASS in my school. With the building principal's consent, half of the students in my behavior program, including Eddie, began to participate in mainstream classes. I spent time with them monitoring their progress and working with the mainstream teachers to support the success of the program. Eddie's outbursts almost immediately decreased to approximately three or four times a month. His success was mirrored by the other students participating in the inclusion approach. At the end of the semester, the building administrator moved all students in our behavior program to the new system.

Eddie continued his journey in learning new ways to manage his anger. Still, his frustration with academic tasks led to inappropriate temper tantrums. Clearly, he understood the new replacement behaviors and could demonstrate them when not enraged, but he was not motivated to use his newfound skills in the most difficult situations. Searching for a reinforcer powerful enough to motivate, I came up with the idea of allowing my students to serve as "aides" to campus staff when their weekly behavior reached higher levels of mastery. Thus, when Eddie improved his anger management, he was allowed to work with the Physical Education teacher or coach when that teacher had classes with younger children. The improvement in his behavior was amazing! Eddie reduced his frequency of aggressive acting out to near zero.

Eddie continued to demonstrate remarkable resilience and sustained behavior change through elementary and junior high. In high school, he received special education services for his learning disability but proudly exited all services for his behavior.

> The least positive thing educators can do is to let a student get away with misbehavior, because getting away with it can be partially reinforcing in and of itself.

It is evident from Eddie's story, and the stories of many school children and young adults with whom we have been privileged to work, that behavior can change when the right set of opportunities is provided. Eddie's story is one repeated in many classrooms but is precious to us because he was there at the beginning.

Hope and I believe that the PASS process, when implemented correctly, can be a forceful agent for change in a student's life because we have seen it happen so often. But success stories paint only a part of the picture. Fortunately, the data we have collected over the years supports our contention.

Does PASS Work?

Schools that implement PASS have seen their students experience increased levels of academic and behavioral success in mainstream settings and observed reductions in the number of students placed in more restrictive environments.

- ✓ Henry Clay High School in Lexington, Kentucky, reported these statistics for its PASS students. Over the course of a year and a half, office referrals were reduced by 86 percent. In one year, in-school suspensions were reduced by 34 percent and suspensions by 54 percent. The daily attendance rate increased by 47 percent.

- ✓ Bryan Station High School in Lexington, Kentucky, reported a 75.5 percent reduction in office referrals, a 94 percent reduction in in-school suspensions, an 89 percent reduction in out-of-school suspensions, and a 67 percent increase in the daily attendance rate for its PASS students over one year.

- ✓ Tate's Creek High School in Lexington, Kentucky, identified a 41 percent reduction in office referrals issued to students participating in their PASS program (Fall semester 2007 vs. 2008).

- ✓ Katy Independent School District in Katy, Texas, observed a 48 percent increase in the participation of their mainstreamed EBD students in the first year of their PASS program (2005-2006 school year).

- ✓ Lamar Consolidated Independent School District in Rosenberg, Texas, reported a 65 percent reduction in discipline referrals for PASS students in their first year of PASS implementation. Over a two-year time period (2004-2006), they observed their EBD students increase mainstream participation by 84 percent.

✓ Fannie Bush Elementary in Winchester, Kentucky, observed a 28 percent reduction in office referrals of PASS students and a 91 percent decrease in suspensions over the course of one year.

✓ Collectively, two high schools and three middle schools in Madison County, Kentucky, saw a 47 percent reduction in suspensions of PASS students after five months of implementation when compared with data from the same period in the previous year.

✓ Galena Park ISD in Houston, Texas, observed a 33 percent increase in the graduation rate of their EBD students in eight years of PASS implementation.

*E*BD Outcomes

✓ Students with EBD are among the least likely to receive mostly A and B letter grades.

✓ Nearly 41 percent score in the low range on direct social skills assessments.

✓ 72.9 percent have been suspended or expelled from school as compared with 32.7 percent of all students with disabilities and 22 percent of same-age students in the general population.

✓ More than one third of secondary students with EBD (34.8 percent) have been arrested—the highest of any disability group.

✓ Thirty percent are in a general education school but outside general education classes for more than 60 percent of the day. Only 19 percent of all students with disabilities are in such settings.

✓ Students with EBD are more than four times as likely to be educated in a separate facility, public or private, than all other students with disabilities.

Bradley, R., Henderson, K., & Monfore, D.A. (2004). A national perspective on children with emotional disorders. Behavioral Disorders, 29, 211–223.

Why PASS?

Why would a school or district change the way it traditionally delivers services to students with behavioral issues (i.e., a levels-system approach)?

The No Child Left Behind Act of 2004 mandates that we educate *all* children, even those with behavior issues. The IDEA amendments of 1997 and 2004 require that we educate those children in the "least restrictive placement." Yet, we are failing to achieve these directives. According to the 23rd Report to Congress, only 57 percent of youth with disabilities graduated with regular diplomas during the 1998-1999 school year (U.S. Department of Education, 2001). And more specifically, Wagner (1995) found that the dropout rate for students with emotional or behavioral disabilities is approximately twice that of general education students.

An article in the *Journal of Behavioral Disorders* (Bradley, Henderson, & Monfore, 2004) provides a review of research regarding the current status of services for children with emotional or behavioral problems. Several investigations summarized in this article found that these students have the poorest outcomes on measures of educational, social, and behavioral competencies of any disability group. Other research reported by Bradley et al. indicates that students identified as EBD are more apt to be placed in restrictive academic settings than any other disability group.

From these findings, it is possible to surmise that restricting students with emotional or behavioral problems to self-contained classrooms does not further their educational, social, or behavioral learning and in some cases causes them to drop out of school entirely. Clearly, a program that provides social instruction in an inclusive setting is needed for these students.

But why choose PASS as that program? There are a variety of reasons why PASS works effectively to provide educational services in mainstream settings to students with behavioral issues.

First, PASS incorporates research-based strategies. For instance, Quinn and McDougal (1998) identified seven practices that constitute best practice in programming for students with EBD. Those criteria are:

- Strict diagnosis and classification

- Screening and assessment for planning and evaluation of services

- Appropriate research-based interventions

Restricting students with emotional or behavioral problems to self-contained classrooms does not further their educational, social, or behavioral learning.

- Effective academic instruction

- Crisis management procedures

- Collaboration among disciplines

- Family involvement

All of these criteria are incorporated into the PASS model set forth in this book.

Second, IDEA (1997) emphasizes the development of Behavior Intervention Plans (BIPs) for students based on Positive Behavior Supports (PBS). While there are many different definitions of PBS, there is general agreement that interventions that focus on the following are supportive of the PBS philosophy:

- Explicitly teaching expectations for academic and behavioral success

- Treating students with dignity and respect

- Working collaboratively

PASS approaches the educational programming of students with EBD from this perspective.

PASS: An Alternative to Levels-System Approaches to Services for EBD

✓ PASS is inclusive. *The majority of PASS services are delivered in the mainstream inclusive setting.*

✓ PASS is constructive. *PASS builds environments and behavioral skills rather than punishment procedures.*

✓ PASS focuses on behavioral education. *PASS provides formal and informal delivery of social skills training.*

✓ PASS stresses a positive approach to behavior management. *PASS emphasizes academic and behavioral success, treating students with dignity and respect and using collaborative team efforts to do so.*

Finally, in a levels-system approach—one in which students pass through a sequentially organized hierarchy of intervention levels that target academic or social behaviors—it is easy to lose individualized instruction. As Scheuermann, Webber, Partin, and Knies (1994) have pointed out, these programs frequently resort to protocols that are common to all participating students. PASS addresses this lack of individualization by combining individually targeted and intensive social skills instruction with behavior monitoring and coaching—attributes identified as best practices in serving youth with EBD (Quinn & McDougal, 1998).

HOW TO USE THIS BOOK

This book describes how to implement a PASS program in your school. As such, it provides information to school and district administrators, teachers (both general and special education), school psychologists, counselors, behavioral specialists—anyone who is or will be involved in designing and implementing PASS.

This chapter, Chapter 2: Overview, and Chapter 3: PASS Staff introduce the program, provide a brief outline of its structure, and define the roles of participants. These chapters will be useful for everyone to read.

Chapter 4: The PASS Classroom defines the purpose of the PASS classroom. It describes the ideal physical environment and delineates the basic classroom procedures for the setting in which you will conduct Orientation, the second phase of the process, and provide for Re-Orientations as they are needed in Phase 3: Maintenance and Inclusion. The PASS specialist, behavior specialists, and paraeducators will find this chapter helpful.

Chapters 5–9 will be most informative for those personnel directly involved in the PASS process. These chapters describe each of the four PASS phases.

PHASE 1: PREPLACEMENT

Chapter 5 describes the procedures for identifying PASS students and placing them into the program. This chapter also deals with establishing a PASS team and how to train this group.

PASS addresses this lack of individualization by combining individually targeted and intensive social skills instruction with behavior monitoring and coaching.

PHASE 2: ORIENTATION

Chapter 6 contains information about the instruction, both behavioral and academic, that students receive while they are in the self-contained PASS classroom.

Chapter 7 describes four procedures that form the strength of PASS:

- Monitoring System

- Redirection Process

- Data Recording Apparatus

- Rewards System

This chapter bridges Orientation and Inclusion and Maintenance because these four procedures are introduced to and practiced by students in Phase 2: Orientation, but not actually implemented until students reach Phase 3: Inclusion and Maintenance. As the reader, you will be exposed to these topics as you read Chapter 6, but they will not be explained fully until Chapter 7. By the time you read Chapter 8, you will understand how each of these procedures work and how they interact with each other.

PHASE 3: INCLUSION AND MAINTENANCE

Chapter 8 explains PASS activities that are put in place to ensure student behavioral and academic success in mainstream classrooms. The chapter describes procedures for how to monitor the student's behavior, redirect the student when necessary, and manage resistant students. It also covers how to plan for student-initiated classroom removals, decide when Re-Orientation is required, begin and end the day effectively, make adjustments at midyear and after holidays, plan for self-monitoring, and decide when to dismiss a student from PASS.

PHASE 4: AFTERCARE

Chapter 9 describes the PASS sponsorship option available to PASS students after dismissal. This option provides a way for PASS students to stay connected to the program and thereby receive ongoing support.

Chapter 10: Handling Emergencies discusses procedures school personnel can put into place to facilitate the handling of emergency situations that involve PASS students. These procedures may augment practices required by state laws regarding the management of potentially dangerous student behavior. Recommendations in this manual should not supplant state mandates.

Chapter 11: Implementing PASS provides information about the steps a school staff takes to put a PASS program into operation, specifically the staff and training required to implement the program with fidelity.

Chapter 12: Supervising PASS provides information that campus and district-level administrators will find helpful. Areas covered in this chapter are:

- Overview of activities that administrators should expect to see during their observations of different phases in the PASS process

- The role of effective communication in PASS programs

- Potential problematic issues that can arise on campuses that implement PASS programs

The PASS CD contains several forms and samples described throughout the text that you may reproduce and tailor for your use. Permission is given to administrators and educators who purchase the book to reproduce any form labeled "Reproducible Form" solely for use in one PASS classroom. Further reproduction is strictly prohibited.

The reproducible forms on the CD are provided in PDF format. They can be printed and filled out by hand. They are also enabled so they can be filled out and saved electronically when opened in Adobe Reader version 6 or above. See the Using the PASS CD.txt file on the CD for more detailed instructions on how to fill out forms using Adobe Reader.

The CD also includes a copy of the *PASS Tracker* software. *PASS Tracker* software is an Excel spreadsheet with embedded formulas that will help you collect and analyze data for each student.

A glossary of terms used in this book is also provided.

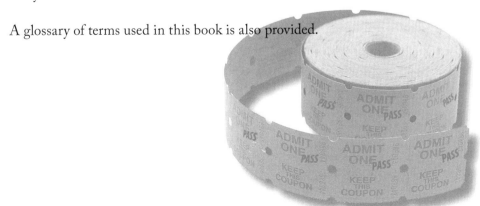

OVERVIEW
The Essence of PASS

PASS provides instruction and support for students with severe behavior problems in mainstream school environments. To achieve this end, we rely on three primary factors:

- A four-phase process

- Trained personnel to facilitate program practices

- A PASS team of collaborating school personnel who use data and FBA (functional behavioral analysis) to support behavioral progress

THE FOUR PHASES OF PASS

PHASE 1: PREPLACEMENT

The first level of PASS focuses on identifying students whose behavior problems have reached the tertiary level of intervention. In the Response to Intervention (RTI) model, students who attain this level of need have participated in previous less intensive interventions without success.

Once a behavioral team has identified a student as a PASS candidate, the next step is to develop a plan that targets two to three of the student's maladaptive behaviors. These become target behaviors (TBs) for PASS intervention.

PHASE 2: ORIENTATION

Direct intervention with identified PASS students begins with an orientation experience. PASS Orientation is a systematic process for providing intensive behavior education in positive, pro-social behaviors that will replace the target behaviors identified in the Preplacement phase.

Orientation activities take place in the self-contained PASS classroom with the PASS specialist, who is typically assisted by one or more paraeducators. The PASS specialist begins by teaching all of the students the behavioral expectations of PASS participation.

All PASS instruction uses a cognitive-behavioral model that emphasizes teacher instruction, teacher modeling, student role-playing, and repeated practice. This applies to teaching behavior expectations in the PASS room as well as to teaching individualized social skills that help each student build replacement behaviors for his or her target behaviors.

During this phase, students and the PASS specialist jointly observe mainstream classrooms to gain further understanding of what it takes to be successful in these settings. Students receive a modified amount of academic work from their mainstream teachers during this phase.

The length of time that each individual student participates in Orientation is typically brief and is determined by completion of Orientation activities.

PHASE 3: INCLUSION & MAINTENANCE

During this third phase of PASS, students attend mainstream classes. PASS staff monitor target behaviors and provide correction and re-teaching of replacement behaviors as necessary. All other behavior issues are managed by the mainstream classroom rules and procedures and the school's student code of conduct.

Data collection centers on the target behaviors, including:

- time
- duration
- antecedents
- consequences

The next step is to develop a plan that targets two to three of the student's maladaptive behaviors.

PASS IN A NUTSHELL

Phase	Purpose	Activities	Who's Directly Involved	Who's Peripherally Involved
1 *Preplacement*	• Identify appropriate students • Identify two or three target behaviors	• Identify student • Refer student • Place student • Identify target behaviors • Identify interventions • Establish teams • Train personnel • Market PASS	• Student • Parents • IEP or school discipline teams • PASS specialist	Administrators, school psychologists, counselors, school nurse, truancy officer, educational diagnostician, social worker
2 *Orientation*	• Intensive individualized social skills instruction • Modified or limited academic instruction	• Explain schedule • Teach expectations • Teach replacement behaviors • Teach PASS monitoring and reward systems • Teach consequences • Teach group social skills • Teach academics • Elicit parent participation • Conduct classroom observation and feedback session • Develop Student Portfolio • Determine readiness • Market PASS student	• Student • PASS specialist • PASS paraeducator • Parents • Mainstream teacher and paraeducator	
3 *Inclusion and Maintenance*	• Monitor student's social/emotional progress in the mainstream class • Correct and re-teach replacement behaviors when necessary	• Monitor • Redirect • Collect & analyze data • Manage resistant students • Student-initiated removals • Deciding on Re-Orientation • Begin and end day • Adjust for midyear and holidays • Plan for self-monitoring • PASS dismissal	• Student • PASS staff • Mainstream teacher and paraeducator • Parents	
4 *Aftercare*	• Supervise and support PASS sponsors and mentees		• Student • PASS staff • Parents	

PASS Tracker software presents a graphic analysis of this data and can be used to further understand the function of the behavior, to tweak interventions, to determine the success or failure of interventions and reward systems, to identify the appropriate monitoring frequency, and to guide decisions regarding the student's move to self-monitoring, program dismissal, or Re-Orientation.

PHASE 4: AFTERCARE

Students who have successfully participated in Phases 2 and 3 of PASS are asked to serve as PASS sponsors for a student who is still in the program. This phase has two goals—ongoing support of the PASS sponsor's behavior change and mentoring for a student currently in the program.

TRAINED PERSONNEL

Implementing PASS requires a school's commitment to select appropriate staff to facilitate the program and then to provide adequate training for that staff.

Usually, one certified teacher serves as the PASS specialist. This teacher is assisted by a paraeducator. As the number of students in the program rises and/or the severity of behavior increases, more paraeducators may be required to provide fidelity to program practices.

The most successful PASS programs are housed in schools that support a team approach to educating all students.

Successful implementation of PASS also requires adequate training for key players. Administrators and program supervisors must have an understanding of PASS philosophy and practices. The PASS specialist and paraeducator(s) must understand the different phases and activities to be completed within each phase. In addition, these individuals must understand the data collection and data analysis process. All school staff members should receive a brief training that highlights the goals of PASS, the monitoring practices, and the roles of different personnel in the PASS process.

THE PASS TEAM

PASS is a collaborative approach to creating behavior education in environments that increase the likelihood of behavior change. The most successful PASS programs are housed in schools that support a team approach to educating all students.

PASS relies on the skills and perspectives of many school specialists on the PASS team. Typically, members of the PASS team include:

- PASS specialist

- School administrator

- Mainstream teachers

- School psychologists and/or school counselor

- Other auxiliary personnel involved in student's educational instruction

- School nurse

- Educational diagnostician

- Truancy officer

- School social worker

- Parents (when issues outside of school appear to affect educational progress)

The PASS team meets regularly to review the data for each student and, if necessary, modify interventions in an ongoing effort to support student success.

A SUCCESSFUL JOURNEY—
One Student at a Time

Jane was a high school student with an emotional/behavioral disorder. She was eligible for special education services and sent to counseling. After several visits, the school psychologist determined that she was struggling with depression, and Jane began weekly sessions.

Despite the counseling sessions, Jane missed 20 days of school in the first semester of the school year. When Jane attended school, she was unkempt and refused to participate in classroom activities. Her interactions with peers were nearly nonexistent. Jane ate alone in the cafeteria. She walked to class by herself, and her only interactions with others were violations of personal space. Jane would push others or confront them by getting within inches of their faces. The IEP committee made a recommendation for PASS services.

In Phase 2: Orientation, the PASS specialist provided Jane with instruction in proper grooming. Jane worked on social skills strategies such as starting a conversation, showing interest in another person, respecting personal space, and appropriate ways to manage conflict.

In Phase 3: Inclusion and Maintenance, the PASS specialist often escorted Jane to class and monitored her frequently. This service was faded as inappropriate target behaviors decreased. Jane's weekly reward for making behavior changes involved working as an office assistant. The office setting, with its high demands for appropriate dress and demeanor, further strengthened her behavior change in targeted areas. The office staff became attached to Jane, and Jane reciprocated. In the following school year, Jane's schedule included daily assignment to the school's front office.

We met Jane when we visited the school to consult with PASS personnel. She escorted us from the front office to a PASS classroom. Along the way, Jane happily chatted with us. She gave us historical information about the school, pointed out awards won by prominent graduates, and greeted others in the hall. We enjoyed Jane's engaging personality. It was only when we arrived at the PASS classroom and the PASS specialist excused herself to talk with Jane that we learned of Jane's history with PASS.

CHAPTER 3

PASS STAFF
Personnel and Their Roles

PASS uses the combined and coordinated efforts of campus and district personnel. For students with behavior problems to succeed academically and behaviorally, key individuals need to understand the function and purpose of PASS as well as their specific roles and responsibilities.

Key players in PASS are:

- Students identified as in need of PASS services

- PASS specialist

- Paraeducator(s) assisting with management of PASS

- General education or special education classroom teachers who provide academic instruction to students

- School administrators

- Counselors and school psychologists

- Auxiliary personnel (school nurse, truancy officer, educational diagnostician, social worker)

- The student's parents or guardians

PASS Students

Students participating in PASS instruction are typically individuals whose misbehaviors have been intractable to previous, less intensive intervention. These students have not responded successfully to any universal-level (preventive activities such as corrective feedback and office referrals) or secondary-level (small group) interventions that the school has in place.

PASS students come from both general and special education. Some school programs are funded by special education and, consequently, student eligibility for program participation hinges on a special education disability (e.g., EBD, OHI, or LD). In such cases, participation in the program is determined at an IEP meeting. In other PASS programs, student participants have been identified as behaviorally at-risk but do not meet eligibility requirements for special education.

PASS Specialist

The PASS specialist is the focal staff member in PASS implementations. This person is a certified teacher whose assignment is the management of students admitted to the program. The PASS specialist is central to the implementation of PASS and the success of students in the program.

A successful PASS specialist knows the basic principles of behavior management and applies a functional approach to understanding behavior. This staff member employs a positive approach to behavior change and interacts positively and patiently with adults and students. A PASS specialist must be flexible and able to stay calm during crises.

Key responsibilities of the PASS specialist include the following:

- Participate in the Preplacement process, particularly in the development of the student's behavior plan.

- Provide behavioral instruction and oversight of academic instruction while the student is participating in the Orientation phase.

- Support the general education and special education teacher(s) with behavior management of students who have returned to their mainstream classrooms.

- Establish and maintain regular daily or weekly parental contact.

- Supervise PASS data collection and analyze data to revise or refine student behavioral instruction.

- Organize PASS team meetings and share student data with team members.

- Provide PASS staff development regarding the PASS program for school personnel and parents.

- Maintain all student and program records.

- Manage crisis situations that involve PASS students.

- Supervise PASS paraeducator(s).

- Establish collaborative working relationships among PASS staff.

- Market PASS and the PASS student to teachers who are new to the system.

PASS Specialist's Role in PASS Phases

Throughout Phases 1–4, the goal of the PASS specialist is to break down barriers to the student's academic and behavioral success in school settings. The specialist promotes academic success by supporting the student in mainstream classrooms where subject-area and grade-level teachers provide academic instruction. The PASS specialist is a highly qualified teacher of replacement behaviors. He or she provides the instruction and practice of these behaviors throughout different phases of the program.

Phase 1: Preplacement. The PASS specialist serves as a consultant in assisting with the identification of appropriate PASS candidates and in developing an appropriate behavior plan.

Phase 2: Orientation. The PASS specialist provides social skills instruction in areas targeted by the student's behavior plan. Toward the end of this phase, the specialist engages each student in a collaborative problem-solving session during a mainstream classroom observation and feedback experience. Before a PASS student leaves Phase 2, the PASS specialist becomes the agent for that student by providing a Student Portfolio to mainstream teachers. The portfolio contains information about target behaviors, replacement behaviors, monitoring schedules, and personal information about the student's strengths and challenges. A critical

The goal of the PASS specialist is to break down barriers to the student's academic and behavioral success in school settings.

role of the PASS specialist is to provide teachers with adequate information and training about PASS services. Of equal importance, the PASS specialist works with the PASS student to clarify and learn how to meet the behavioral expectations of the classroom teacher.

Phase 3: Inclusion and Maintenance. During this phase, the PASS specialist is primarily responsible for re-teaching replacement behaviors in the natural or mainstream setting. In addition, the specialist (along with the PASS team) engages in weekly behavior analysis and intervention planning as PASS students are observed and data is collected. PASS personnel also maintain student records, including behavior analysis charts generated by the *PASS Tracker* software, monitoring data, School-to-Home notes, PASS Room Logs, and Student Portfolios. The accompanying CD contains samples of many of these items. See Appendix B for a listing of the CD's contents.

Phase 4: Aftercare. The primary role of the PASS specialist in this phase is to organize and supervise PASS sponsors—those students who have been dismissed from formal PASS services but who remain connected to PASS by mentoring students in Phases 2 or 3. We have found that mentoring other PASS students helps PASS sponsors maintain behavior stability. The PASS specialist sets up meetings and supervises interactions between PASS sponsors and their mentees.

THE PASS PARAEDUCATOR

The paraeducator's role in PASS is critical. PASS programs are always staffed with at least one PASS specialist working in coordination with an assistant.

Like a PASS specialist, a successful PASS paraeducator demonstrates personal maturity, has a history of positive interactions with children, and communicates effectively. The paraeducator is patient and able to maintain calm in a crisis.

Working collaboratively with the PASS specialist, the paraeducator supports the management of the PASS classroom and the monitoring of student behavior in mainstream classrooms. Fidelity to PASS practices is a key component of the paraeducator's role. Toward this end, the PASS paraeducator should receive detailed training in all PASS procedures. Responsibilities typically include:

• Maintain student records, including the daily School-to-Home parent note and updates to the Student Portfolio.

• Supervise student behavior in common areas such as the lunchroom and restroom.

- Monitor mainstream settings and redirect target behaviors.

- Assist PASS specialist in Orientation and Re-Orientation activities.

- Monitor student medication schedules.

- Assist in management of student crises.

- Input PASS monitoring data into *PASS Tracker* software.

The consistency with which PASS staff provide services to students is critical for student behavior change. Ensuring that expectations for PASS operations are taught to staff is the responsibility of the PASS specialist. Adhering to these expectations is the hallmark of an effective paraeducator.

GENERAL EDUCATION AND SPECIAL EDUCATION CLASSROOM TEACHERS

General education and special education teachers are primarily responsible for academic instruction. These teachers are also responsible for encouraging appropriate classroom behavior and for correcting misbehavior *not* targeted on the student's behavior plan. As with all students, the campus code of conduct and the teacher's classroom rules should inform practice. PASS students should receive the same encouragement and consequences as their nondisabled peers for behaviors not identified on the student's behavior plan.

For those behaviors identified as target behaviors on the student's behavior plan, mainstream teachers are responsible for the following:

- Deliver the first corrective intervention to a misbehaving student—e.g., "Harry, please leave the lab area and return to your assigned seat."

- Use a PASS monitoring token to indicate the acceptability level of student target behaviors.

- Provide the student a fresh start after removal from the classroom for a redirection by PASS staff. This includes use of monitoring tokens as described in Chapter 7.

The consistency with which PASS staff provide services to students is critical for student behavior change.

In addition, mainstream teachers serve on the PASS team and meet periodically to analyze a student's progress using PASS data and to problem-solve areas of concern.

Mainstream teachers are key to the success of PASS students. Positive classroom management of all students and a calm, matter-of-fact demeanor support the success of PASS students. Nowhere is this more evident than in the mainstream teacher's management of crisis situations and handling of the student's re-entry to the classroom following a crisis or redirection.

The partnership between PASS and mainstream teachers is essential. Ideally, they will agree on classroom management techniques and share an understanding that a problem-solving approach to behavior creates an environment in which behavior change can occur.

MAINSTREAM TEACHERS PROVIDE
Normal Childhood Experiences

James was in sixth grade. He had been in self-contained EBD classrooms since kindergarten for his aggressive behavior issues. When he reached the sixth grade, he was placed in PASS. He progressed through Orientation and entered Phase 3: Inclusion and Maintenance.

His mainstream teacher organized a field trip to a local park. To heighten the sense of adventure, she bought all of her students a pair of binoculars from the Dollar Store. The class brought sack lunches and spent an enjoyable day exploring the park and the adjoining lake.

When it came time to leave, the teacher counted heads and realized that one student was missing. She frantically searched the area and finally found James sitting calmly by the lake, binoculars in hand.

"James," she rebuked. "I was worried sick! Everyone is supposed to stay together on a field trip. Haven't you ever been on a field trip before?"
James looked at her with utter bewilderment. "No, Ma'am," he said.

> The partnership between PASS and mainstream teachers is essential.

SCHOOL ADMINISTRATORS

In schools staffed with both a principal and assistant principals, roles differ in regard to participation in the PASS program. The typical approach on a campus with multiple administrators is for an assistant principal to take responsibility for overseeing the program and PASS personnel. This person plays a key role within the PASS program. In many instances, it is the assistant principal who provides backup for the PASS specialist and paraeducator during student crises.

In addition, the designated PASS administrator serves on the student's PASS team. His or her signature on team meeting invitations often ensures staff attendance. The principal's administrative support is also important should a problem with staff management of identified students occur.

Perhaps the most important role that any administrator can take with the PASS program is support for PASS practices and philosophy. This support is conveyed by administrators who do the following:

- Actively participate in training the entire campus on PASS goals and practices.
- Attend PASS team meetings.
- Convey a problem-solving approach to student behavior management.
- Ensure that PASS staff follow procedures with fidelity and that mainstream teachers provide the behavior support delineated on the student's behavior plan.

More details on the supervision of PASS are found in Chapter 12.

COUNSELORS

Counseling in support of the student's behavioral progress is frequently a very important component of student success. Research supports a cognitive-behavioral/behavioral counseling approach in assisting students with aggressive acting-out behavior. Successful counseling programs for these students often emphasize anger management and the development of positive interpersonal skills. Schools differ on who delivers this service, but often choose between the school counselor, a special education counselor, or a school psychologist.

As with other individuals on the PASS team, communication between the counselor and other professional personnel involved with the student is imperative.

SCHOOL PSYCHOLOGISTS

School psychologists are typically involved at two levels. Prior to placing a student in PASS, many schools identify the need for a behavior consult and/or psychological

evaluation to assess the appropriateness of a PASS placement and/or to conduct an FBA to guide in the development of an appropriate behavior plan. After a student is placed in PASS, the school psychologist's participation on PASS teams is extremely helpful as the teams analyze behavioral data and modify or add interventions.

AUXILIARY PERSONNEL

Other school personnel may support the positive behavior of PASS students. The school nurse, school truancy officer, educational diagnostician, and school social worker may participate on PASS teams as required by an individualized behavior plan. If a student needs medication, for example, the school nurse will be most able to clarify the behavioral consequences of the medication. If attendance is an issue, the truancy officer may be invited to a staff meeting regarding that behavior. In states where educational diagnosticians assess for learning issues and understand the consequences of specific learning problems, a diagnostician may be included on a team when a PASS student demonstrates problems with academics. Social workers with access to community agencies and resources are frequently key players in developing successful programs.

PARENTS

PASS views parents and guardians as partners in the delivery of educational services for their child. Establishing this partnership is frequently a difficult task. Contact with parents may be difficult when parents work and/or may be absent from the home. At times, parents of PASS students have had so many negative interactions with school personnel that they become defensive or hostile, or avoid school contacts entirely.

Despite these difficulties, parents of students identified for program services must be included in all phases of the program. In the Preplacement phase, parents may provide critical insight into the student's behavioral history and patterns of behavior. During Orientation and Inclusion and Maintenance, the parent's support of PASS goals will improve the student's chances for positive behavioral change.

PASS staff can enhance their likelihood of positive relationships with parents by communicating with parents early in PASS programming when their student demonstrates positive behaviors. (See Reproducible 3-1, an informational letter about PASS, on the following page). This early, and frequent, communication with parents has proven to be successful in gaining parental support and trust. PASS staff can also encourage parental support by offering guidance for behavioral problems that occur in the home. Over time, PASS personnel and families can jointly effect long-term behavioral improvement—often at school and in the home.

SCHOOL TO HOME—
Home to School

In his first semester of PASS, Samuel's very aggressive behavior diminished, but his maladaptive behaviors re-emerged second semester. His regression included verbal outbursts directed toward PASS personnel, teachers, and students. Staff called Samuel's parents to schedule a home visit or a meeting at school.

Samuel's father answered the phone but quickly passed the call to Samuel's mother. They arranged to meet at school, but only the mother appeared. While discussing Samuel's regression, his mother reported that his behavior was also deteriorating at home. He had become more aggressive, particularly toward younger siblings. In response, the parents had increased corporal punishment. His mother also reported the recent death of Samuel's favorite grandmother.

With the mother's consent, staff invited the school counselor to the meeting. Together they developed a plan of action. Samuel's mother agreed to try the plan for a month.

At school, Samuel would participate in weekly counseling meetings. His mother would discontinue corporal punishment for the month. Instead, she would use the PASS Monitoring System with him. Staff provided PASS monitoring tokens and directions for their use. Samuel's mother agreed to respond to the daily School-to-Home note and indicate the appropriateness of home behavior in the targeted areas. They agreed that they would collect data on the incidence of targeted behaviors both at home and at school. The PASS program agreed to incorporate this data into the PASS Tracker *and* Reward System. *On days when the School-to-Home note indicated behavior above and beyond expected limits, a bonus/reward would be provided early in the school day. The PASS specialist scheduled a meeting with Samuel and explained the plan.*

Within a two-week period, data indicated a decrease in aggression both at home and at school. At the next meeting with Samuel's parents, both mother and father attended. Pleased with Samuel's progress, the parents were receptive to information about community counseling services for the entire family.

Reproducible 3-1 *The PASS Program: A Positive Approach to Student Success*

The PASS Program: A Positive Approach to Student Success

REPRODUCIBLE
3-1

PASS *(Positive Approach to Student Success)* provides behavior education services to students with emotional and behavioral issues. The primary setting in which these services are provided is the mainstream classroom. PASS is founded on the belief that youth benefit behaviorally from educational experiences with their appropriately behaved peers and academically from participation in the general curriculum.

With the ongoing support of a PASS specialist, each student in PASS learns, practices, and implements individualized strategies that address targeted behaviors of concern. The program is implemented in four phases:

(1) Preplacement

(2) Orientation

(3) Maintenance and Inclusion

(4) Aftercare

Phase 1 incorporates activities prior to PASS placement, such as ensuring that less intensive and restrictive interventions have occurred, developing a behavior plan that targets the two or three behaviors that interfere most with the student's academic and behavioral progress, and formal placement in PASS by either an IEP committee or school behavior team.

In Phase 2, the primary PASS focus is on behavior education. Instruction is provided on PASS classroom expectations, the PASS monitoring and reinforcement systems, and social skills in the area(s) targeted by the student's behavior plan. In this phase, students complete a modified amount of academic work provided by mainstream teachers. Orientation is brief and individualized. The setting for these services is the PASS classroom.

Phase 3 moves the student from the PASS classroom into mainstream settings. Monitoring and coaching of student behavior occurs on a schedule designed to meet the needs of individual students. Reinforcement of behavioral success is a key component of this phase, and social skills instruction/coaching continues. After a period of behavioral success with PASS personnel providing monitoring, students move on to self-monitoring.

Movement by the student through the second and third phases of PASS is not linear. Rather, the level of services students receive is fluid and dependent on their current behavioral needs. Students may, therefore, move from PASS monitoring back to the PASS classroom for a period of Reorientation and/or from PASS monitoring to self-monitoring. Data gathered during monitoring is analyzed and informs the level of service provided throughout these phases.

Phase 4 of PASS is an Aftercare experience. Students who have successfully "graduated" from PASS are offered opportunities to serve as PASS sponsors and work with other students currently in Phase 2 or 3 of PASS.

PASS is a collaborative effort by all key stakeholders in a student's school life. Parents, administrators, the PASS specialist, mainstream teachers, and others partner in their efforts to effectively support behavior change.

The PASS specialist working with your student is identified below and may be reached at the contact number provided.

PASS Specialist _Mr. Smith_   Contact information _555-2121, call before_

8 am and between 3 and 3:30 pm

CHAPTER 4

PASS CLASSROOM
Philosophy and Organization

While PASS is primarily an inclusive approach to the management of students with behavior issues, there remains a need for a physical classroom. The second phase of PASS—Orientation— occurs within this setting. When students move on to Phase 3: Inclusion and Maintenance, the PASS room functions as a center for Re-Orientation, additional or supplemental social skills training, certain reinforcement activities, and crisis de-escalation.

There may be times when PASS students want to use the PASS classroom as a way to avoid unpleasant tasks or consequences. Therefore, students can never *voluntarily* return to the PASS classroom. Because the objective of PASS is to help students develop problem-solving strategies in natural settings, the PASS classroom can be viewed as an educational environment, but one that is not so rewarding and comfortable that the student chooses to stay rather than exit to the inclusion setting.

Two uses of the PASS classroom are incompatible with PASS philosophy.

First, on occasion schools have attempted to concurrently run a PASS program and use the PASS setting and personnel to run an in-school suspension (ISS). An initial staff misconception may be that PASS is a timeout room or disciplinary placement for students with a disability. This distorts the appropriate use of the PASS classroom as an educational setting for Positive Behavior Supports and prevents PASS personnel from providing appropriate PASS instruction. It also diminishes their ability to monitor and assess behavior and to redirect PASS students when their target behaviors are exhibited in mainstream settings. To address this issue, it is important to educate all staff regarding the function of PASS.

Second, the PASS classroom may also be misused as a center for Phase 3 PASS students to do makeup work for their academic classes. If students need help with academic work or additional time to complete assignments, the PASS specialist should redirect the student to a setting designed for this purpose, such as a content mastery or resource classroom. However, if a student is in behavioral crisis, the behavioral team may suggest that the student return to the PASS classroom for Re-Orientation. In this case, the general education teacher is expected to oversee academic assignments and make frequent contact with the student about classwork while the student is in the PASS classroom.

CLASSROOM ORGANIZATION

The Physical Environment

An effective way to facilitate a PASS student's return to the mainstream classroom is to keep the PASS room as sterile and neutral as possible while emphasizing the rewards and the appeal of the inclusion setting. For example, the only items on the wall of the PASS classroom are posters that indicate students' progress toward reinforcement goals or posters with classroom rules and expectations. Graphic material and social skills posters from programs such as *Second Step* are also consistent with the goal of identifying the educational purposes of the PASS classroom.

Keep the PASS room as sterile and neutral as possible while emphasizing the rewards and the appeal of the inclusion setting.

The size of the environment is another issue to consider when establishing a PASS classroom. Consideration should be given to the number of students that the program serves and the intensity level of misbehavior exhibited by program participants. The room should be large enough so that teachers can use a "divide and conquer" approach to maintaining adequate space between acting-out students.

Procedures

A PASS schedule should be established and posted. The schedule is generic and applies to all students participating in Orientation or Re-Orientation. An effective schedule includes the following:

- Frequent changes in activity (that is, the activity changes every 15 to 30 minutes depending on the age, maturity, and attention level of students participating in the program)

- A mixture of various types of educational activities through-out the school day (for example, direct instruction, social skills activity with opportunities for role-play, and independent seat work)

We use the *CHAMPS* model (Sprick, 2009; Sprick, Garrison, & Howard, 1998) for teaching PASS classroom behavioral expectations. Within this framework, we give students explicit instruction in five areas of classroom activity:

Conversation: Conversing

Help: Asking for help

Activity: How behavioral expectations vary across activities

Movement: Moving about the room

Participation: How to display participation in classroom activities

Success: Soar to success

PHASE 1
Preplacement

PHASE 1:
Preplacement → **PHASE 2:** *Orientation*

PHASE 4: *Aftercare* ← **PHASE 3:** *Inclusion & Maintenance*

P hase 1 of the PASS program includes all activities initiated prior to the PASS student's actual participation in program services. Phase 1: Preplacement activities include:

- Identifying PASS candidates

- Referring a student

- Formally placing a student

- Programming for transfer students

- Determining target behavior(s) and appropriate interventions

- Establishing PASS team

- Training team members

- Marketing PASS

IDENTIFYING PASS CANDIDATES

Candidates for PASS instruction are students highly at-risk for school failure with histories of severe misbehavior that persists despite diligent attempts to provide Positive Behavior Supports to remediate that behavior.

To clarify, consider these two students:

Sally...

- is a high school student who missed 50 days of school by close of the second grading period.

- may be homeless and/or a runaway.

- frequently fails to complete homework or come to class with materials.

- is often rude to teachers and substitutes and often ignores requests.

- has never participated in campus interventions such as counseling.

- has never been involved in interventions with auxiliary personnel.

Harry...

- is a fourth-grade student who struck a teacher on two different occasions.

- frequently tantrums with little apparent cause.

- has a psychiatric history with one recent hospitalization.

- has been suspended on three occasions during the current school year.

- has participated in group anger management with the campus counselor as part of an intervention plan.

Figure 5-1 *Three Levels of Intervention*

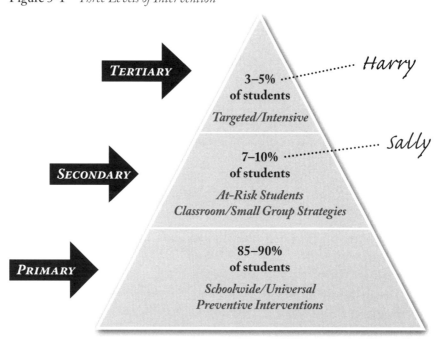

Which of these students qualifies for PASS?

If you said Harry, you would be correct. Harry is an ideal candidate for PASS services. His behavior is aggressive and occasionally violent, he has a psychiatric history, and the school has provided small-group intervention to no avail, as indicated by his suspension record. Clearly, Harry falls in the tertiary level of intervention.

Sally, on the other hand, is at risk of school failure, but her rudeness and inattentiveness to school tasks can be explained by other factors. Because she has yet to be included in campus interventions or involved with auxiliary personnel, she may well be served on the secondary level without the need for targeted and intensive strategies such as PASS.

Typically, but not always, PASS students have been identified as meeting special education criteria such as EBD or OHI. When dealing with special-needs students, it is important to note that provision of a Free and Appropriate Education (FAPE) carries with it the legal responsibility for IEP teams to review the individual student's needs to determine what services and educational settings are appropriate. Though PASS instruction is individualized, *not every identified student can be appropriately served by PASS* or within mainstream settings. Some students may require more restrictive settings to receive appropriate educational services.

A school or district can also provide PASS services to general education students. Several school districts combine special education and general education funds to finance PASS services so that they can provide these services to students with disabilities and also to general education students with severe behavior problems.

REFERRING A STUDENT

Referral for consideration of PASS services may come from a variety of sources:

- A student may be referred by a school student assistance team (SAT), the Individual Education Plan (IEP) team, a 504 committee, or problem-solving committee involved in the school's Response to Intervention (RTI) process.

- A school psychologist or counselor may refer students.

- Parents or guardians may refer students.

Not all students referred to PASS through these sources may be determined to be appropriate candidates for PASS. It is the formal placement team that makes placement decisions.

Though PASS instruction is individualized, not every identified student can be appropriately served by PASS or within mainstream settings.

Formally Placing a Student

The IEP team formally places a student with a special education disability into PASS. When placing a general education student, schools frequently use a problem-solving committee.

Many school districts require that a school psychologist evaluate a student before PASS placement to determine whether less intensive and more appropriate interventions can be delivered within the mainstream setting. If the school psychologist finds that the school has made and documented interventions that proved unsuccessful in changing the maladaptive behavior, consideration of PASS services becomes appropriate.

In districts where the services of a school psychologist are not available, the school counselor, educational diagnostician, special education department head, or an administrator assigned to special education issues may perform the role of facilitator in PASS placements.

Programming for Transfer Students

In many cases, students considered for PASS are transfer students from other schools and other school districts. In these instances, school district policies regarding matching educational services should apply.

Identify only two or three behaviors as targets for PASS intervention so as not to overwhelm the student and staff.

DETERMINING TARGET BEHAVIORS AND APPROPRIATE INTERVENTIONS

When an IEP, problem-solving, or RTI team determines that PASS services are appropriate for a specific student, they must then make critical decisions regarding the identification of maladaptive behaviors to address for intervention. We recommend that they identify only two or three behaviors as targets for PASS intervention so as not to overwhelm the student and staff. Other less critical behaviors can be addressed once the student has success with these two or three target behaviors.

When selecting specific behaviors for intervention, the team may wish to consider these guidelines:

- Deal with dangerous behaviors first.

- Order other misbehaviors from the most disruptive to the student's educational progress to the least disruptive. Target for early intervention those behaviors that interfere most significantly with the student's success in school settings. Remember to consider academic, behavioral, and emotional issues.

- Identify the replacement behavior for each maladaptive behavior listed.

Mark was a third-grade student whose behavior had become so severe that he was frequently sent to the front office for disciplinary action. Mark had a history of acting-out problems. In the previous school year, there were reports that he cried and refused to work when given assignments. When Mark was referred for PASS, his reading/language arts teacher reported that whenever he was presented with an independent work assignment, he refused. With independent assignments, he typically wadded the paper up or tore it into pieces. When his teacher attempted to address these behaviors, Mark ran out of the room to the busloading area and had, on occasion, left school grounds without permission. Mark had an excellent relationship with the assistant principal. When approached outside the classroom, Mark generally responded to the assistant principal's request to follow her to the front office. In the office, Mark obligingly assisted the secretary with tasks such as making copies on the office copier and delivering notes to other classrooms.

In identifying target behaviors for remediation, it is important to consider the functional aspects of these behaviors for the individual student. Functional assessments that identify the antecedents, setting events, and maintaining consequences surrounding the problem behavior(s) are vital to the referral team's development of an effective behavior plan for the student.

Data indicated that Mark's target behaviors occurred almost exclusively in the morning during reading and language arts instruction. In addition, staff observed that the incidents of Mark leaving the class without permission increased whenever the consequence was an extended period in the front office. The team hypothesized that the function of Mark's behavior was avoidance. Further, they concluded that office referrals were actually reinforcing Mark's behavior rather than punishing it.

(continued)

The problem-solving team made a decision to refer Mark to PASS. The team identified target behaviors for intervention as:

1. *Leaving class and/or school without permission*

2. *Destruction of schoolwork*

The replacement behaviors the team identified as behavioral goals for Mark were as follows:

1. *Ask or signal the teacher for help with frustrating tasks.*

2. *Practice self-calming exercises such as deep breathing or counting to ten, then backwards to one.*

3. *Use a Stop, Think, Plan approach to problem-solving.*

Eventually, as a reward system for using replacement behaviors, Mark's successes would earn him a job in the office.

Many resources are available to assist teams in developing intervention plans. In Mark's situation, we used *The Teacher's Encyclopedia of Behavior Management* (Sprick & Howard, 1995) and specifically the chapter "Self-Control Issues: Problems with Anger Management."

ESTABLISHING A PASS TEAM

Best practice dictates that instruction for students with an emotional disturbance be planned and facilitated collaboratively (Quinn & McDougal, 1998). PASS specialists facilitate communication about student issues by establishing a PASS team for each PASS student. This team meets regularly, reviews behavior using data provided from the *PASS Tracker*, and uses a problem-solving approach to discuss interventions that are likely to facilitate student progress in academic and behavioral areas.

The PASS team membership typically consists of:

- PASS specialist

- School counselor or school psychologist

- School nurse (if medication issues are relevant)

- General education and/or special education teacher(s) serving the PASS student for whom the meeting was called

- Principal or assistant principal

The function of the PASS team is to facilitate the delivery of those interventions identified on the student's behavior plan. In addition, this team monitors student progress toward behavioral goals using data collected by PASS personnel.

The team also has the important responsibility of monitoring the student's affective or emotional status and facilitating an appropriate response to changes in the student's needs. Decisions about a student's return to the PASS classroom for Re-Orientation or referrals to additional mental health services are examples of decisions typically made by this team. However, it should be emphasized that when a student is in crisis, immediate responses to that crisis should be the first priority—not calling a team meeting.

Training Team Members in Their Roles

PASS team members should be trained in the PASS model before the student's re-entry into the mainstream classroom. At a minimum, team members should know and understand:

- How to use the PASS Monitoring System

- How the mainstream teacher is expected to manage PASS student behavior

- How to implement intervention strategies identified by the behavior plan

- What the crisis response procedures are

- Any other information about the student's functioning that is important for instruction and for monitoring the student's behavioral or emotional status

Furthermore, all team members, especially mainstream teachers, need to understand that the goal in Phase 3 is for students to return to their mainstream classrooms as quickly as possible following their removal for redirection of inappropriate behavior. PASS is *not* a disciplinary setting designed to punish students by removing them to a restrictive setting for inappropriate behavior choices.

All team members, especially mainstream teachers, should understand that PASS students who are removed from the classroom for redirection return to the mainstream classroom when:

- The student verbalizes or demonstrates to PASS personnel the appropriate replacement behavior.

PASS is not a disciplinary setting designed to punish students by removing them to a restrictive setting for inappropriate behavior choices.

- The student indicates his or her willingness to make the appropriate behavioral choice on return to the mainstream setting.

- The student displays affective or emotional control.

Mainstream teachers must agree that when students return to mainstream classrooms, they have a clean slate in those settings. Successful re-entry can be impaired when students are met by a teacher who is hostile or wishes to further punish them.

It is particularly helpful when training teachers about redirection to role-play an inappropriate method of handling a student's return to the classroom. For example, play the role of the classroom teacher who meets a PASS student at the classroom door with hands on hips and a frown and, in a very strict voice, says, "Well, young man, I hope you learned your lesson not to disturb my class. I've been teaching 45 years in this building, and NOBODY gets away with that kind of disrespect." Then model an appropriate approach—when the student returns to the classroom, the teacher turns the monitoring token to green, approaches the student's desk, and says in a private voice, "Tim, glad to have you back. We're now on page 30."

Another use of role-play in training PASS team members is to illustrate behaviors they can expect to see during the course of the school year and provide them with management strategies to deal with anticipated problems. Role-plays should approximate the level and intensity of misbehavior likely to be exhibited.

Don't exaggerate misbehavior in these role-plays as it can lead to the idea that anticipated misbehavior is more severe than it is and create an unnecessarily negative perception of the student.

MARKETING PASS

Before placing students in mainstream classrooms, it is particularly important to *market* the PASS behavior management approach to school personnel. An accurate representation of what administrators and teachers may expect from participation is critical. For example, mainstream teachers must know they will have ongoing support in the management of a student's misbehavior within their classrooms. PASS staff initially provides this with frequent (every 5 to 15 minutes) classroom visitation or monitoring. It is also reasonable for the mainstream teacher to anticipate that the PASS specialist will consult with teachers about classroom management strategies for reducing the misbehavior of students not formally participating in PASS.

Marketing PASS and training staff is essentially the same thing. If the PASS specialist has adequately prepared mainstream staff by presenting information about the program, modeling and role-playing techniques, and providing answers to questions, the mainstream staff will be more accepting. As time goes on, if mainstream staff perceive PASS staff as helpful in managing difficult behavior in their classrooms, they increase their buy-in to the program.

More information about training staff is found in Chapter 11.

CHAPTER 6

PHASE 2
Orientation

PHASE 1:
Preplacement

PHASE 2:
Orientation

PHASE 4:
Aftercare

PHASE 3:
Inclusion & Maintenance

Phase 2: Orientation begins after the following steps occur:

1. An IEP/RTI/problem-solving team makes a formal decision to provide the student with PASS services.

2. The team identifies target behaviors and appropriate interventions.

3. The PASS specialist forms and trains the PASS team.

The primary emphasis in Phase 2 is on behavioral instruction. The PASS specialist focuses on facilitating the student's development of appropriate replacement behaviors for maladaptive behaviors that interfere with his or her behavioral and academic success in school. Concurrently, the mainstream teacher visits the student in the PASS classroom to provide and support limited academic activities.

Orientation activities are divided into two categories: early and late. Early activities take place in a segregated PASS classroom. Late activities occur after a student has demonstrated an understanding of PASS expectations and procedures and has attained affective control. At this stage, the student and specialist move into mainstream classrooms for brief periods to observe and discuss behavioral expectations within those settings.

TEACH, MODEL, ROLE-PLAY, AND PRACTICE BEHAVIOR

Early Orientation activities include:

- Explaining the PASS schedule

- Teaching PASS expectations

- Teaching replacement behavior(s)

- Teaching the PASS Monitoring System

- Teaching the PASS Reward System

- Teaching students about PASS consequences for inappropriate behavior

- Teaching group social skills

- Teaching academics

- Eliciting parent participation

Late Orientation activities include:

- Conducting classroom observation and student feedback sessions

- Developing the Student Portfolio

- Determining readiness for entry into mainstream classroom(s)

- Marketing the PASS student

As with every aspect of PASS, a student's participation in Orientation is individualized. One student may spend a week in Early Orientation activities and move quickly into later tasks, while another student may spend two or three weeks attempting to master early-phase activities. Students new to PASS are often initially resistant to requirements for behavioral change. Therefore, the first few weeks of a student's participation in PASS are often challenging for both the specialist and the student. To encourage success during this period, staff should:

- Be consistent. This applies to all the adults managing the student's behavior.

- Be calm. Use a matter-of-fact, nonemotional approach to the management of student misbehavior.

- Be proactive with instruction. Maintain a focus on teaching and practicing replacement behaviors, not on reacting to misbehavior.

The specialist's role in these early weeks of PASS is directed toward establishing both authority and trust.

EARLY ORIENTATION ACTIVITIES

Explaining the PASS Schedule

A schedule of PASS activities during Orientation should be posted and explained to students. When developing the schedule, keep in mind that effective schedules feature frequent changes among a variety of activities. This is a typical PASS schedule.

8:00–8:20	Direct instruction in PASS expectations
8:20–8:40	Practice in PASS procedures
8:40–9:10	Independent seatwork in academics
9:10–9:40	Behavior education (group/individual)
9:40–9:50	Restroom break
9:50–10:10	Direct instruction in PASS expectations
10:10–10:30	Practice in PASS procedures
10:30–11:00	Independent seatwork in academics
11:00–11:30	Lunch
11:30–11:40	Restroom break
11:40–12:00	Independent seatwork in academics
12:00–12:30	Behavior education/role-play experiences
12:30–12:50	Direct instruction in PASS procedures
12:50–1:10	Practice in PASS procedures
1:10–1:40	Independent seatwork in academics
1:40–1:50	Restroom break
1:50–2:20	Reward activity for students at 80 percent or more of appropriate behavior
2:20–2:40	Direct instruction in PASS expectations
2:40–2:50	Practice in PASS procedures
2:50–3:00	End-of-day wrap-up activities

Staff Innovation

Some PASS staff make a practice of copying daily schedules for each student and placing the schedule on students' desks. As students complete a task, they mark off the activity to gain a sense of accomplishment.

Following the posted schedule is paramount during the Orientation phase. The goal is to establish a structured and predictable environment within the PASS classroom from the outset. It is important for students to understand that instruction will occur regardless of any behavior problems they exhibit during this period.

Teaching PASS Expectations

The first task of Phase 2: Orientation is to provide explicit instruction on program expectations for student behavior during all PASS activities. For example, students need to understand what to do during independent seatwork, how to exit and re-enter the mainstream classroom after misbehavior, and what behaviors are expected during restroom breaks.

Using the CHAMPS behavior management model (Sprick, 2009), the PASS specialist identifies and teaches expectations for specific activities in five areas. Expectations should clarify:

> ### Staff Innovation
>
> At a suburban high school in Texas, the PASS specialist has his Orientation students prepare a PowerPoint lesson on PASS expectations. These students teach their lesson to other PASS students or to PASS staff.

Conversation:	Can students talk to each other?
Help:	How do students get their questions answered? How do they get the teacher's attention?
Activity:	What is the task or objective? What is the end product?
Movement:	Can students move about?
Participation:	What does the expected student behavior look and sound like? How do students show they are fully participating?
Success:	Soar to success!

For example, using this model, PASS personnel might teach the following behavioral expectations for lunch period:

Conversation:	Talk in low tones to your neighbor.
Help:	Ask for assistance by raising your hand.
Activity:	Eat your lunch neatly and calmly.
Movement:	Stay in your assigned seat until dismissed by a PASS staff member.
Participation:	Put all of your lunch things away and wait for dismissal. When a PASS staff member releases you, put your trash in the trash receptacle as you exit the cafeteria.
Success:	Great job!

Using the CHAMPS framework, staff can develop other lessons for behavioral expectations during such activities as social skills instruction, behavioral instruction by the teacher or paraeducator, independent seatwork, riding the bus, and bathroom behavior.

Teach PASS expectations in small instructional units that always include:

- Direct instruction—an explanation of expectations
- Demonstration
- Role-playing
- Corrective feedback
- Positive descriptive feedback

Provide multiple opportunities for drill and practice. Ask students to demonstrate their understanding by writing or creating drawings that illustrate expected behaviors. By the end of the first week in Orientation, a student may be expected to successfully complete a test on the rules and expectations of the PASS classroom. However, to enhance confidence, any test should be modified to match the student's academic level.

Beyond establishing order and clarity of behavioral expectations within the PASS classroom, this activity has one other very important objective. Students learn that though expectations may vary across classrooms, *every* classroom has behavioral expectations. They also learn that expectations may be less clearly and directly communicated in some classrooms. At the end of Phase 2: Orientation, each student, with the help of the specialist, will define the expectations of the mainstream classroom(s) they will enter.

Teaching Replacement Behavior(s)

The primary goal of Orientation is to teach students alternative pro-social behaviors to replace those that have interfered with their educational success. Staff uses the student's behavior plan as a guide for identifying these targeted replacement behaviors.

Students learn that though expectations may vary across classrooms, every classroom has behavioral expectations.

TEACH, MODEL, ROLE-PLAY, AND PRACTICE BEHAVIOR

PASS provides behavior education through the following steps:

- Teacher, with the student, develops T-charts that identify the positive and negative examples of targeted behaviors.

- Teacher models the positive appropriate replacement behavior.

- Student role-plays the replacement behavior.

- Teacher uses a reward system to acknowledge successful displays of the replacement behavior.

T-chart development is always a cooperative task between the specialist and the student. We believe it is best to begin by asking the student to identify personal examples of the targeted inappropriate behavior. Once these maladaptive behaviors have been identified, the student typically needs more assistance from the specialist in identifying alternative pro-social responses. See Figure 6-1 for examples.

Figure 6-1 *T-chart Examples*

TARGET BEHAVIOR #1: PHYSICAL AGGRESSION TOWARD PEERS

Unacceptable Behaviors	Replacement Behaviors
▪ Hitting, kicking, fighting, or wrestling	▪ I could keep my hands and feet to myself. (student generated)
▪ Biting, scratching, or spitting	▪ I could walk away. (student generated)
▪ Throwing things	▪ I could belly breathe or count.
	▪ I could find an adult to mediate.

TARGET BEHAVIOR #2: RUNNING AWAY FROM ASSIGNED AREA

Unacceptable Behaviors	Replacement Behaviors
▪ Running out of the classroom	▪ When I start to feel my face flush and my heart beat quickly, I will ask to see my safe person.
▪ Running out of the school building	▪ I could belly breathe.
▪ Running off campus	▪ I could count backwards by threes.

TARGET BEHAVIOR #3: VERBAL AGGRESSION

Unacceptable Behaviors	Replacement Behaviors
▪ Cursing at my peers and teachers when angry	▪ I could belly breathe.
▪ Yelling and cursing when frustrated with my classwork	▪ I could say words that are not curse words. (replacement words)
▪ Yelling and cursing when needing help with my work	▪ I could ask a teacher for help.

Once T-charts are complete, the PASS specialist demonstrates or models the appropriate behavior. It is not uncommon for adults to feel uncomfortable with these demonstrations. Even so, the specialist must demonstrate appropriate behaviors to communicate his or her belief that this behavior is appropriate. Students quickly pick up an adult's discomfort and interpret it as "They think this behavior is dumb, so why should I do it?" The specialist can diffuse discomfort with humor: "I'm not going to get an Academy Award for this demonstration, but you might try something like this . . ."

Next, the specialist asks the student to role-play the appropriate response as just demonstrated. If a student balks or describes the behavior as dumb, we use the technique of going with the resistance rather than fighting it. We say something like, "Look, you've got to fake it to make it." These types of statements tell the student that new behaviors often feel artificial and fake, which normalizes their discomfort. On another level, we feel that while behaviors may initially not be genuine, they are likely to become an internalized part of the student's behavioral repertoire if they are practiced and rewarded enough.

Role-playing also provides students with a mirror in which to view their inappropriate behavior and its consequences, including its impact on others. If possible, schedule times when other students can role-play with students who are in Orientation.

> ## Sample Role Play
>
> The student has just helped the PASS specialist develop a T-chart on Verbal Aggression (see Figure 6-1).
>
> **Specialist:** OK, I think we have a good list of replacement behaviors for your cursing. Now let's think about situations in which you might try out these behaviors.
>
> Watch me while I demonstrate how you can substitute a word that's OK to use in school for a curse word. Let's say your teacher tells you to rewrite your science project. This is how you could handle that: "Oh, bummer! That's going to take a lot of time."
>
> Now, I'll be your science teacher. Let's see you handle this same situation.

With younger students, PASS specialists sometimes use sock puppets in role-playing. Students can make or use different puppets to represent faculty members on the campus or a peer with whom they have difficulty.

The final step in developing a replacement behavior plan is communicating to the student "what's in it for them" if they engage in new pro-social behavioral choices. We use a reward system to motivate students to use appropriate replacement behaviors. In PASS, rewards are tied to successful mastery of the targeted behaviors identified on the student's behavior plan. The reward system is integrally related to the PASS Monitoring System.

Teaching the PASS Monitoring System

During Phase 2: Orientation, students are introduced to and practice the PASS Monitoring System in preparation for their participation in the mainstream classroom. Activities for learning how to use the Monitoring System include:

- Introduce students to monitoring tokens that indicate whether the student's behavior is acceptable, needs improvement, or warrants removal and redirection.

- Role-play to practice replacement behaviors when the monitoring token indicates that behavior needs improvement.

- Role-play to practice how to leave the classroom when the monitoring token indicates behavior is not acceptable and redirection is required.

- Role-play to practice how to re-enter the mainstream classroom.

- Explain how monitoring data translates into rewards.

Though the PASS Monitoring System is not officially used during Orientation, ample opportunity exists for students to learn how the system works. So, in effect, PASS staff use the system unofficially to provide practice. This unofficial monitoring of student behavior during Orientation has two benefits beyond that of learning the system. First, there are opportunities for students to experience frustration when behavior is judged to be inappropriate and to practice socially acceptable methods for dealing with that frustration. Second, students learn the benefits of appropriate behavior through a PASS Reward System before they enter the classroom program.

During Phase 3: Inclusion and Maintenance, the student, mainstream teacher, PASS specialist, and paraeducator use the monitoring system collaboratively. The PASS Monitoring System is an essential tool for ensuring students' behavioral success. It is described in greater depth in Chapter 7.

Teaching the PASS Reward System

The PASS Reward System encourages student buy-in and keeps students moving in a positive, productive direction once they are in a mainstream classroom.

During Phase 2: Orientation, the PASS specialist explains the system in preparation for its use in Phase 3. Students learn:

- How to earn rewards (items such as school supplies and valued responsibilities and jobs)

- The hierarchy of rewards

- Who delivers rewards

The PASS Reward System is also an essential tool to a student's behavioral success. It is described in greater depth in Chapter 7.

Any rewards provided during Phase 2 Orientation should be small. They are not tied to the official PASS Reward System. The rationale for keeping rewards at a minimum during Orientation reflects the goal of moving students back into the mainstream as quickly as possible. If students view Orientation as rewarding, there is a danger that they will want to stay in the PASS classroom. Hence, rewards, if given, should be insignificant compared with the rewards that students may earn in their mainstream classes.

Teaching Students About Consequences

The focus of PASS is on addressing and stopping problem behavior before it starts through targeted interventions and direct instruction in alternative pro-social behaviors. While students are in the process of learning new behaviors, they also learn that there is a consequence when target behaviors are not appropriately replaced. Consequences for acting-out include:

- Failure to earn credit toward mastery and rewards

- Corrections

During Phase 2: Orientation, PASS students learn to correct their behaviors through acts of restitution. Restitution in PASS involves two actions: an apology followed by an act of amends—an action to repair damage to the relationship and address the behavior that needs correction. Restitution carries the message, "If you broke it, you fix it." As a result, many PASS consequences involve a restitution of some type. *Restitution: Restructuring School Discipline* (Gossen, 1998) is a useful resource for developing effective restitution.

While students are in the process of learning new behaviors, they also learn that there is a consequence when target behaviors are not appropriately replaced.

TEACH, MODEL, ROLE-PLAY,
AND PRACTICE BEHAVIOR

Case Study

During Orientation, the PASS specialist asks Harry to put away his car magazine and return to an independent work assignment. Harry throws the magazine down and yells obscenities. In this case, two consequences occur.

First, the PASS specialist changes Harry's token to yellow and gives him two or three minutes to comply. When Harry refuses, the specialist changes the token to red. (In the mainstream classroom, changing a token to red would reduce Harry's credit toward mastery in the PASS Tracker, but this does not apply in Orientation.) Harry is then taken out of the room for redirection. The PASS specialist waits until Harry is calm—possibly walking out his anger.

Second, when Harry displays affective control, he is asked to return to the PASS classroom where, in a private meeting, he will practice restitution. If Harry does not know how to apologize, the PASS specialist will model and have Harry practice. Next, Harry will learn how to ask to perform some act of amends. Typically, amends are actions tied to the misbehavior for which they are performed. The specialist and Harry will discuss options such as asking if he can make up the lost academic time during his lunch.

During Phase 3: Inclusion and Maintenance, the timing and delivery of consequences become critical variables in their effectiveness. See Chapter 8 for more information on consequences once students are their mainstream classes.

In situations where students' acting-out behavior becomes a danger to themselves or to others, PASS programs must be aware of and adhere to state guidelines regarding the use of restraint techniques. The guiding principle in these situations is to use restraint *only as a last resort* to protect the acting-out child or others from physical harm. Trained and certified personnel should administer restraints. Many programs are available that train participants in techniques of de-escalation. We highly recommend that PASS personnel focus on identifying crises situations early in their development so that they can defuse them.

The guiding principle in these situations is to use restraint only as a last resort to protect the acting-out child or others from physical harm.

note

De-escalation techniques differ depending on the program (for example, Crisis Prevention Institute) and are very specific. Hence, we do not offer an example of a de-escalation technique, but rather defer to the school's selection of approach.

Teaching Group Social Skills

Phase 2: Orientation does provide an opportunity for social skills lessons on behaviors of benefit to all PASS students. Because the majority of students who typically receive PASS services have externalizing behavior, we recommend that PASS programs consider *Second Step: A Violence Prevention Curriculum* (Committee for Children, 2002). *Second Step* is a research-based program for the reduction of aggression and the promotion of social competence. *Second Step* provides a scripted curriculum supported by visual prompts that PASS specialists have found easy to use.

Second Step

Second Step: A Violence Prevention Curriculum is designed to reduce impulsive and aggressive behavior in children by increasing their social competency skills. The program comprises three grade-specific curricula: preschool/kindergarten (Pre/K), elementary school (grades 1–5), and middle school (grades 6–8). The curricula are designed for teachers and other youth service providers to present in a classroom or other group setting. For more information, go to www.cfchildren.org.

A decision about the use of PASS to provide social skills programming is a campus- and/or district-level one due to the debate on the efficacy of group social skills instruction. Maag (2005) points out that research regarding the positive impact of social skills on behavior change in students identified as emotionally or behaviorally disordered has been mixed. He suggests that the emphasis of social skill instruction be placed on the development of replacement behaviors, and it is this approach that PASS endorses. In addition, other researchers have reported the potential for negative outcomes in grouping students with disruptive disorders (Arnold & Hughes, 1998; Dishion, McCord, & Poulin, 1999).

Teaching Academics

As noted earlier, the primary focus of Phase 2: Orientation is to instruct students in replacement behaviors. Nevertheless, some level of academic instruction should be provided. Designing the PASS schedule to provide behavioral instruction and enough academic instruction to keep the student from falling behind educationally is a balancing act.

Provision of academic services is a cooperative endeavor between the PASS specialist and the student's teacher of record in the mainstream setting.

During PASS Orientation, the mainstream teacher provides modified assignments for the student to complete in the PASS classroom. Assignments are

TEACH, MODEL, ROLE-PLAY, AND PRACTICE BEHAVIOR

typically shortened to accommodate instruction in behavior. In addition, students who meet criteria for any other special education disability may have academic work modified according to their academic IEPs. Because mainstream teachers may be uncertain about the amount of work to provide, an agreement between the specialist and teacher to allow the specialist to determine the appropriate amount of work completion is an effective approach. It is, of course, the role of the specialist to communicate with the teacher about all academic issues.

During Phase 2, the mainstream teacher meets with the student in the PASS classroom several times. Alternatively, PASS personnel may accompany the student to the mainstream classroom during the teacher's conference period. These meetings are designed for two purposes.

First, the student can begin to develop a positive relationship with the teacher before entry into the mainstream classroom. Teachers can facilitate this relationship by dropping by the PASS classroom to check on the student's progress, by indicating an interest in the student's success, and by conveying a desire to see the student in the mainstream classroom. This is also an excellent opportunity for the teacher of record to discuss expectations and rules for behavior that apply in the mainstream classroom.

Second, these interactions offer the mainstream teacher an opportunity to provide instruction in problematic academic areas and ensure that the student understands his or her assignments.

During Phase 2, the mainstream teacher meets with the student in the PASS classroom several times.

To facilitate the mainstream teacher's participation in Orientation, the PASS paraeducator may supervise the mainstream classroom for a brief period. For instance, the teacher may assign independent seatwork for a brief period (for example, 15 minutes). The paraeducator can then oversee this activity while the teacher works with the PASS student in the PASS classroom.

The PASS specialist's role in academic instruction is to facilitate completion of work assigned by the mainstream teacher. This may include occasional tutoring and brief instruction. During academic tasks, it is important to maintain boundaries for students about who is in charge of their academic education. To prevent confusion, refer to the mainstream teacher as "your teacher" and the PASS specialist as "your behavior support specialist."

The PASS specialist should also observe the level of academic competency and any problematic behaviors that students display when working on academic assignments. For instance, the specialist

Sample Modification Plan

Harry's independent seatwork will be limited to 20-minute periods.

can identify tasks a student avoids and those that elicit frustration, observe the number of times a student re-starts a particular task, record the amount of time a student stays focused on specific assignments, and iden-tify a student's strongest vs. weakest and favorite vs. least favorite subjects. This information constitutes valuable in-formation that the team can use in successfully program-ming for the PASS student.

Sample Observation Note

On days when John's medica-tions have not been provided at home, his handwriting deteriorates.

During this phase, the PASS specialist also works with the student's PASS team. The specialist may display a student's work and share observation notes gathered while the student is in Orientation. At this time, the team begins collaborative problem-solving to determine how to modify academic instruction in the main-stream setting. Modifications should enhance the likelihood of a student's master-ing the academic curriculum while reducing the probability of triggering behavior problems with frustration.

Eliciting Parent Participation

During the first week of orientation, the specialist should make the time to devel-op a positive relationship with parents of the PASS student. Frequently, the PASS specialist must work on re-establishing parent-school relationships that have de-teriorated over time.

Remember, PASS is a fresh start for the parents as well as the student.

Here are some helpful strategies for developing relationships with parents:

- Contact parents by phone early in the PASS process with posi-tive feedback about their child's participation and strengths.

- Ask the parent of younger students to actively participate in activities such as a Fun Friday reward activity.

- Emphasize the collaborative approach to behavior by inquiring about behavioral changes the parent would like to see at home and offering suggestions about positive approaches to managing that behavior.

- Educate parents in the use of the PASS School-to-Home Note (see Reproducible 6-1 on the next page) and how their student can earn bonus tokens toward rewards for appropriate behavior in targeted behavioral areas at home.

Reproducible 6-1   *PASS School-to-Home Note*

Print from CD ▶

School-to-Home Note

REPRODUCIBLE 6-1

Parent or Guardian: As a part of the school and home partnership in educating your student, this communication will be sent home daily. Please review, sign, and return the following school day. Signed notes and reports of appropriate home behavior will contribute to mastery credit your student earns toward rewards. If you would like to communicate additional information, please do so on the back of this form, or contact your PASS specialist by phone or e-mail.

Student _Jamie P._

PASS Specialist _Mr. Smith_   Phone _555-1212_   E-mail _cjsmith@ourschool.edu_

Target Behaviors for your student are:
TB #1 _verbal aggression toward peers_
TB #2 _work refusal_
TB #3 _stealing_

		MONDAY	TUESDAY	WEDNESDAY	THURSDAY	FRIDAY
Mastery of Target Behavior(s)						
	Good 80%		X			
	Average 60–80%	X		X		
	Poor - 60%					
Remained in Class						
	Yes	X	X			
	No			X		
Homework						
	Yes		X	X		
	No	X				
Teacher Comment on Back						
	Yes		X	X		
	No	X				
Parent Comment on Back						
	Yes					
	No	X	X			
Behavior at Home						
	Good	X				
	Average		X			
	Poor					
Parent Signature		Ann Jones	Ann Jones			

© 2009 James R. Poole and Hope Caperton-Brown | *Reproducible Form*

Visits to the student's home are another way of establishing a working relationship with parents. Parents tend to respond positively during home visits because they are on their own turf. Also, the specialist has the opportunity to assist the parent by helping set up a program within the home that reflects the goals of PASS. An important recommendation that the specialist may make to the parent is to decide on a specific location where the child can place the PASS School-to-Home note when he or she gets home. The parent is encouraged to always check this site, sign the form the next morning with an assessment of home behavior, and then return the folder to the same site each time for the student to pick up when leaving for school.

Visits to the student's home are another way of establishing a working relationship with parents.

It is always advisable for a specialist to check with campus administration about school policies that govern visits to students' homes. For example, we suggest that PASS personnel always schedule home visits in advance. In addition, staff should never visit a student's home alone. Always make arrangements for another faculty member or administrator to accompany you.

LATE ORIENTATION ACTIVITIES

Conducting Classroom Observation and Student Feedback Sessions

Late in the Orientation phase, the specialist determines whether the PASS student's behavior has reached a level of stability and readiness that will allow the student to enter mainstream settings for a structured observation of the class. Readiness considerations may include evaluations of the following PASS classroom behaviors.

- Does the student exhibit appropriate behavior in regard to PASS expectations?

- Does the student demonstrate appropriate replacement behaviors?

- Does the student understand behavioral expectations for entering and leaving mainstream classrooms?

An additional factor to consider in regard to a student's readiness is affective stability. Is the student demonstrating the ability to manage inappropriate emotional displays?

If all of the above criteria are met, the PASS specialist schedules an observation of a mainstream classroom(s) with the mainstream teacher(s). The number of observations scheduled for each PASS student will vary. Factors to consider in determining the number of observations an individual student may need include:

- The student's age

- The level of anxiety a student has about entering mainstream classrooms

- The variety of classroom settings that are judged to be potentially problematic for the student when he or she enters Phase 3: Inclusion and Maintenance

PASS students in middle or high school generally return to all of their mainstream classes after Orientation. On occasion, depending on the needs of a particular student, we begin with one or two classes and move the student into other classes gradually over time. But this is less common.

TEACH, MODEL, ROLE-PLAY, AND PRACTICE BEHAVIOR

Typically, an elementary student observes his or her mainstream classroom(s) at least two times prior to Phase 3. Observations should occur at different times of the day and during instruction in different subject areas. A secondary student may observe two or more classes.

Prior to the observation, the PASS specialist preps the student on elements of the classroom structure to observe. Specifically, the student is asked to use the CHAMPS (Sprick, 2009; Sprick et al., 1998) framework, making notes on classroom expectations regarding:

- When conversation with other students is acceptable

- How students ask for help

- How specific expectations vary across activities

- What the rules are for freedom of movement around the classroom

- What is expected regarding student participation in specific activities

In addition, the specialist asks students to observe the behavior of other students within the classroom and assess the potential for those students to be helpful or harmful to their success in that setting. Younger students may need an abbreviated list of items to observe, and several observation sessions may be scheduled for them.

Reproducible 6-2 on the opposite page shows a sample PASS Classroom Observation Form.

Observations are short in duration—no more than 15 minutes—and are always immediately followed by a student feedback session during which the specialist queries the PASS student:

- What did you think of the class?

- What did you observe regarding classroom expectations?

- Any worries about being in this class?

The student's responses to the above questions should give the specialist a sense of the positive or negative attitude the student has toward this setting, the student's ability to perceive classroom expectations, and any worries or anxiety the student has about being a student in this classroom.

Reproducible 6-2   *Classroom Observation and Student Feedback Form*

Classroom Observation & Student Feedback Form

PASS Student: You are about to observe one of the classrooms where you will soon be a student. Please use this form to record your observations about classroom behavior expectations in this setting.

Class Observed *Social Studies*   Date *11/6*

Time: From *9:45* to *10:00* (Remember, observations should be no more than 15 minutes.)

What activity was the class engaged in at the time of the observation? *teacher lesson/small grp discussion*

1. Is it OK to talk with other students during this activity? When is it OK to talk?

    No talking when the teacher is teaching, unless you raise your hand to answer a question. It is OK to talk to other people in your group when the teacher says so. You should talk about the assignment, not about anything else.

2. How do students ask their teacher for help in this class?

    They raise their hand. If a group has a question, they should keep working until the teacher comes over.

3. If the activity changed during observation, did classroom rules for behavior change? If so, describe the change(s).

    Yes. When the teacher is teaching, there is no talking and no leaving your seat. When you are working in a group, you can talk to the others in your group. You can get up if you need to sharpen your pencil or get paper or a book to look something up.

4. Is it OK to get up out of your desk and move around the room during this activity?

    Not when the teacher is teaching. During group work, you can go to the pencil sharpener, the supply shelf, and the book shelf.

5. How does this teacher expect students to participate in the observed activity?

    During small groups, you should listen to what other people say and be a part of the group talk. If your job is to take notes, you should write down what the group talks about or their answers to the questions. When the teacher is teaching, you should listen to what he is saying. Be ready to raise your hand to answer questions. You should take notes in your notebook and be sure to write down the homework assignment.

Negativity toward the class or worries about the class that the student expresses should be followed by problem-solving interactions between the specialist and the student.

The last question regarding a student's concerns about the classroom is particularly important to ask. It is not uncommon for a student to identify old rivals, girlfriends, or previous problems with this teacher during the feedback session.

Negativity toward the class or worries about the class that the student expresses should be followed by problem-solving interactions between the specialist and the student. For example, if a student indicates that he anticipates problems from an ex-girlfriend in the class, the specialist might ask, "How could you handle that situation without creating a problem for yourself?" The student offers strategies first and the specialist follows up with additional strategies *only* when the student's suggestions are not likely to be beneficial. It is not appropriate to tell students that they should not feel as they do or to offer false reassurance that what they fear will never happen.

Students who have difficulty describing the classroom rules or expectations may need assistance from the specialist. The specialist might say, "Well, let me tell you what I observed. I saw Ms. M correct a student who went to the pencil sharpener during her lecture. So I don't think it's OK to move around the room when she's talking."

As an alternative, the mainstream teacher can conduct the feedback session. In this case, the specialist might supervise the mainstream classroom while the teacher and PASS student go to a private place and the teacher asks, "What did you observe regarding classroom expectations?" The teacher can clear up any misconceptions at that time.

The PASS team may want to consider a class change if a student demonstrates very strong opposition and/or concerns about his or her ability to be successful there. Interventions may include placing the student in other settings that appear more appropriate or introducing more behavior education in coping with anticipated problems.

Developing the Student Portfolio

During the time the student is in orientation, the PASS specialist should be developing a student profile folder, which is given to the mainstream teacher *before* the student begins the inclusion process of Phase 3. The Student Portfolio should be a recipe for success in mainstream settings. A sample Student Portfolio is included on the CD.

The following items are typically included in the Student Portfolio:

- Copies of the student's IEP/BIP if the student is in special education or a copy of the general education student's behavior plan

- Student schedule (e.g., class, counseling, group social skills, medication, and reinforcement times)

- Suggested behavior management strategies appropriate for mainstream classroom application

- Definitive work samples

- Mandated modifications to academic work

Typically, the first resources that the specialist consults in developing the Student Portfolio are the behavior plans developed by the referral committee responsible for the student's PASS placement. If the student participates in special education, a psychologist's recommendation, found in a comprehensive individual assessment, is included. It is also helpful to record any successful strategies the specialist used during the orientation period. Plans from *The Teacher's Encyclopedia* (Sprick & Howard, 1995) are useful in this regard.

Work samples from PASS Orientation or work assessment observations gathered during Orientation will also be helpful. These provide the teacher with a model of the type of work the student has the potential to perform and are particularly informative when paired with an example of work where the student did not perform to his/her potential. Certain information is always useful—length of time the student requires to finish specific tasks, how much assistance the student requires on specific types of coursework, and any modifications the specialist may have provided on the assignment.

The specialist is responsible for providing updates to the student's portfolio during the school year. Therefore, it is important that the all portfolios be present during PASS team meetings as well as during IEP meetings if the student participates in special education.

Determining Readiness

The specialist should consider several important variables in determining if a student is ready to return to mainstream classes. The PASS term for student re-entry is *readiness*. As is true when judging a student's preparedness for classroom observations, readiness to enter the mainstream classroom is demonstrated when:

- The student demonstrates appropriate replacement behaviors as alternatives to the maladaptive behaviors targeted on the behavior plan.

- The student understands the monitoring and rewards systems.

- The student understands behavioral expectations for entering and leaving mainstream classrooms.

Transition to Phase 3—Readiness

1. Student demonstrates understanding of:
   - PASS procedures
   - Replacement behaviors
   - Mainstream class expectations

2. Student demonstrates affective control.

In addition, a student demonstrates readiness by affective stability. Students should not be introduced to mainstream settings when angry, obviously depressed, seriously anxious, or fearful. Students who have not been in mainstream settings before will feel some level of anxiety. In these cases, readiness can be facilitated by acknowledging concerns and helping the student problem-solve to find solutions to his or her fears.

Readiness is not equated with mastery. PASS is not a levels system where a student must earn a certain number of points or attain a specific percentage of appropriate behavior prior to re-entry to mainstream educational settings.

Our rationale for moving students quickly into mainstream settings is supported by research, which highlights the difficulty of effecting generalization of behavior from self-contained settings or social skills groups to mainstream settings. Empirical studies (DuPaul & Eckert, 1997) provide more support for intervention at the point of performance (especially for students with ADHD), and this is the PASS approach in Phase 3.

Once a readiness decision has been made, *it is crucial to ensure that the mainstream teacher understands PASS practices before the student enters the room.*

Readiness is not equated with mastery.

For example, the mainstream teacher needs to be comfortable with and aware of:

- PASS monitoring schedules

- Use of monitoring tokens by the teacher

- What to expect in a redirection

- How to manage the PASS student's return to the mainstream classroom following a redirection

- His or her role in PASS team meetings

- The use of PASS monitoring data

- How to manage crisis situations

- Ways to communicate with the PASS team in addition to monitoring token information

We have found that it is best to meet with the teacher face to face. Such meetings allow PASS staff to model interactions and the teacher to ask questions and/or voice concerns. It is particularly important to prepare the mainstream teacher for behaviors to be ignored (e.g., a student who is unable to sit still for prolonged periods of time or a student with verbal tics).

Decisions regarding the specific class or classes and the number of classes that a student will initially re-enter in Phase 3 should be individualized. Typically, students return to all their mainstream classes at once; however, there are occasional exceptions. The team may decide it is best for a particular student to return to mainstream settings by entering one class at a time. This may happen, for instance, if a student is extremely anxious about re-entering the mainstream.

Marketing the PASS Student

Though most educators probably do not consider themselves experts or experienced in marketing, it is important for PASS specialists to develop skills in marketing the students in the program. Teachers with little or no experience with students with EBD—or those who have familiarity only with segregated, self-contained EBD programming—are frequently apprehensive about an inclusive approach.

Experience has shown that this apprehension is best addressed by a PASS specialist who "walks the walk." In other words, as we introduce the program and discuss monitoring of the student in the mainstream setting, we *must* be consistent in providing the promised level of monitoring. If we say, for example, that we will monitor a particular student an average of every 10 minutes, it is imperative that we do so. If we assure teachers that an acting-out student who is disrupting the delivery of instruction will be removed until the student regains affective control, we must remove that student.

Another approach to dealing with teacher apprehension about students placed in their classroom is to humanize the child. Too frequently, these students have reputations that precede them and that exaggerate their behavior or the disorder underlying their behavior. We help teachers perceive the student as an individual, rather than a diagnosis, by developing a Student Portfolio with specific information about the student's strengths, and, perhaps, about the student's disability. It is the PASS specialist's responsibility to ensure that all teachers participate in a staff meeting where these portfolios are disseminated and detailed information about the student is shared. This occurs prior to a PASS student's placement in the mainstream classroom.

As we introduce the program and discuss monitoring of the student in the mainstream setting, we must be consistent in providing the promised level of monitoring.

BRIDGING PROCEDURES
Monitor, Redirect, Record, Reward

The PASS Monitoring System, redirection procedure, data collection, and Reward System are all interconnected, as illustrated in Figure 7-1 on the following page.

Each of these procedures is introduced to students and, where appropriate, practiced while students are in Phase 2: Orientation. These procedures are fully implemented in Phase 3: Inclusion and Maintenance.

The interrelationship of monitoring, redirecting, recording, and rewarding follows this sequence:

1. Monitoring

PASS staff periodically monitor the student unobtrusively.

If the student is behaving appropriately with respect to his or her target behavior, the token remains on green.

If the student is not behaving appropriately with respect to his or her target behavior, the token is changed to yellow. PASS staff pause to see if the student engages in self-correction.

Figure 7-1   *Interrelationship of PASS Orientation Components*

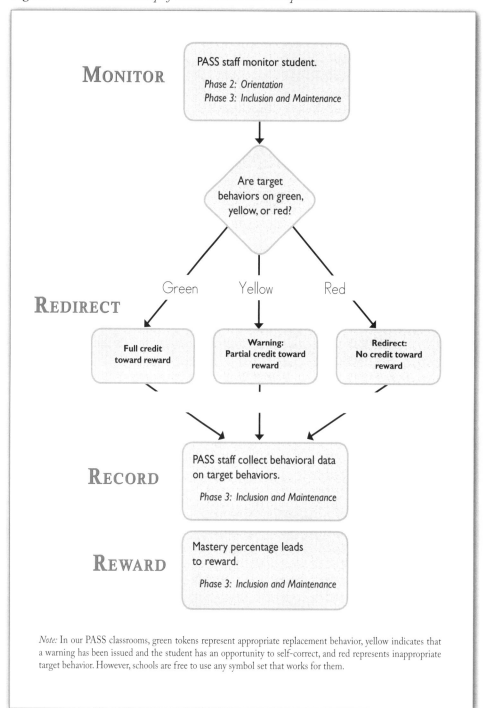

MONITOR

PASS staff monitor student.

Phase 2: Orientation
Phase 3: Inclusion and Maintenance

Are target
behaviors on green,
yellow, or red?

Green   Yellow   Red

REDIRECT

Full credit
toward reward

Warning:
Partial credit toward
reward

Redirect:
No credit toward
reward

RECORD

PASS staff collect behavioral data
on target behaviors.

Phase 3: Inclusion and Maintenance

REWARD

Mastery percentage leads
to reward.

Phase 3: Inclusion and Maintenance

Note: In our PASS classrooms, green tokens represent appropriate replacement behavior, yellow indicates that a warning has been issued and the student has an opportunity to self-correct, and red represents inappropriate target behavior. However, schools are free to use any symbol set that works for them.

Redirecting

If the student does not self-correct and the token goes to red, PASS initiates a redirection. Any time a student's behavior is on red, a PASS FBA Worksheet should be completed (Reproducible 7-1). Staff gather information regarding the antecedents and environmental consequences of the behavior on the PASS FBA Worksheet.

2. Recording

Whether behavior is appropriate or inappropriate, PASS staff record information on the PASS monitoring form.

3. Rewarding

At the end of the week, students earn rewards based on their mastery of target behaviors (TBs) as defined by the data on PASS monitoring forms.

Reproducible 7-1 *PASS FBA Worksheet*

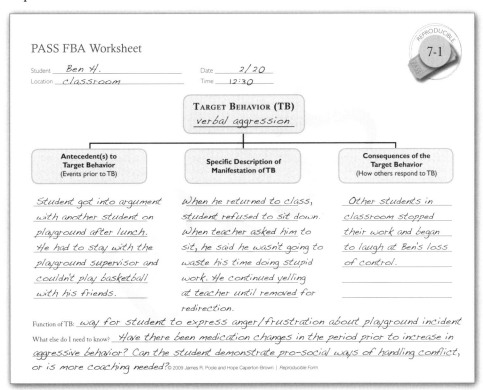

M onitoring Student Behavior

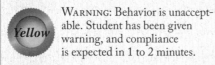

Green — Behavior is acceptable.

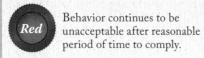

Yellow — WARNING: Behavior is unacceptable. Student has been given warning, and compliance is expected in 1 to 2 minutes.

Red — Behavior continues to be unacceptable after reasonable period of time to comply.

Blue — BONUS: Student has performed above and beyond expectations.

- Mainstream teacher uses monitoring tokens to identify three levels of acceptability of student target behavior(s).

- PASS specialist/paraeducator records the level of behavior at monitoring time and uses data to further the functional assessment of the target behavior.

- PASS personnel redirect behavior at the warning or unacceptable level.

PASS MONITORING SYSTEM

The PASS Monitoring System is extremely important to a student's behavioral success. The system provides immediate feedback and support to the student. Therefore, it is critical that the student and all the teachers involved are trained in the use of the Monitoring System before the student enters the mainstream classroom. Consistency between student and teacher expectations is a crucial variable to the student's success with the PASS program.

The PASS monitoring procedure serves to regulate student behavior during class with the least amount of classroom disruption. Keep in mind that the Monitoring System covers *only behaviors targeted by the student's behavior plan, or BIP.* All other behaviors fall under the school code of conduct.

The PASS monitoring procedure serves to regulate student behavior during class with the least amount of classroom disruption.

PASS Monitoring Tokens

PASS uses a *tangible monitoring system* of tokens to prompt acceptable levels of student behavior.

Schools have used poker chips, blocks, flip charts, felt circles, school mascots painted in different colors, and other innovative items for tokens. Regardless of the monitoring item used, it should be consistently implemented across all students and teachers within the school.

Monitoring tokens should be produced in four colors:

- One color indicates appropriate behavior.

- A second color warns students that they are displaying a target behavior and cues them to engage in replacement behavior.

- A third color indicates noncompliance despite a mainstream teacher's correction or warning and results in an out-of-classroom redirection by PASS staff.

- A fourth color indicates a bonus.

In our PASS classrooms, we use green, yellow, red, and blue tokens, as shown on the previous page.

The token system is best used for one student at a time. If two or more PASS students are in a classroom, each student should have a set of tokens. Different token shapes, or numbers or letters on the tokens, can be used to clarify ownership. Ideally, no more than two PASS students are assigned to any mainstream class at one time. In the case of multiple PASS students in the same classroom, we encourage teachers to use a "divide and conquer" strategy to separate these students physically. When group work occurs, maintaining the separation is vital, as is providing the PASS students with work groups populated with appropriate peer models.

Initially, the PASS specialist delivers monitoring tokens to the mainstream teacher, along with instructions for their use, during the face-to-face meeting that accompanies delivery of the Student Portfolio. Mainstream teachers must know their responsibilities and how to use the monitoring tokens before a student is transitioned. Reproducible 7-2 shows an example of a PASS handout that explains the use of monitoring tokens.

Green Monitoring Token

Green, posted by the mainstream teacher, indicates that the student is not currently displaying a target behavior. The only PASS response to this posting is to record the data on a PASS monitoring form.

It is important that mainstream teachers understand that green does not indicate that *all* student behaviors are appropriate. The student may be misbehaving in an area that violates a classroom rule or the student code of conduct and still be on green.

Reproducible 7-2　*How to Use Monitoring Tokens*

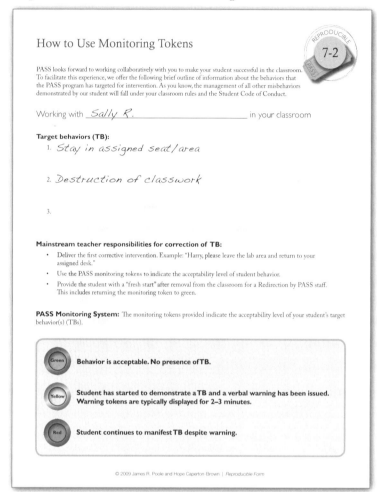

Yellow Monitoring Token

The yellow monitoring token may be the most important token in helping the student develop self-management skills. The token goes up when the mainstream teacher first observes the student engaging in one of his or her target behaviors. The posting of the token is accompanied by a teacher warning and a specific direction about the appropriate behavior. For example, Jamie's teacher may say, "Jamie, you are out of your area and need to return. Take out your math book and complete the exercise on page 11."

Yellow signals a warning that the student is off track and that self-correction should occur within a one- to three-minute period. During this time, the student has been taught to think through the replacement behaviors that he or she collaboratively developed (with the T-chart) and practiced in Orientation.

If a mainstream teacher is reluctant to use yellow and allow a period for self-correction, PASS staff can encourage its use with a traffic light analogy. The teacher would be very unhappy to get a ticket for running a red light if the yellow light never appeared or flashed for an inappropriately brief period of time.

Red Monitoring Token

Red tokens are the mainstream teacher's communication that a target behavior is present, that the student was warned and given time to self-correct, and that the behavior has continued. It signals the PASS monitor to remove the student from the mainstream classroom for a redirection.

PASS Bonus Token

The final monitoring token, indicating that a student has performed above and beyond expectations, is the *bonus token*. This is the blue token.

Bonus tokens may be delivered to the student by the PASS specialist, PASS paraeducator, mainstream teacher, a member of the academic or behavior team, administrator, or any staff member trained in their use and who has regular contact with the student.

Students earn a bonus token when they demonstrate positive behavior above and beyond demonstrations of replacement behaviors. The PASS team should determine behaviors that merit bonus tokens. Examples of student actions that deserve a bonus token include:

- Positive notes from parents reporting that home behavior in the targeted areas has been acceptable

- Acts of restitution

We encourage staff to award most bonus tokens for student restitutions. When a student performs restitution in PASS, he or she:

- Apologizes to the injured party.

- Performs some action to make amends.

Opportunities to earn bonus tokens are critical to the program's success. They offer a student who has "lost it" early in the week an opportunity to regroup and earn a reward later in the week. Bonus tokens mitigate the likelihood that students give up midweek and consequently experience a behavioral decline. The opportunity to redeem oneself also communicates an important message—it is always possible to recover from a poor behavioral choice.

Students earn a bonus token when they demonstrate positive behavior above and beyond demonstrations of replacement behaviors.

"You broke it, you fix it."

This principle guides restitution and focuses not just on repairing tangible items but also on repairing broken relationships.

PASS staff typically prompt students to perform restitution after their behavior has gone to red and they have been removed for a redirection. No student can be forced to perform the restitution tasks. However, incentive in the form of regaining lost credit toward mastery is provided to motivate students.

Some students easily come to decisions about what act of amends they would like to perform. Others have more difficulty and need PASS recommendations.

Case Study

In a situation with a high school student who had a loud verbal altercation with one of his teachers, a subsequent conversation between the student and PASS specialist yielded the following plan. In addition to apologizing for the inappropriate language and manner of handling the disagreement, the student decided that he would bake the teacher a cake! This very athletic male student bought a cake mix after school, arranged with the home economics teacher to come in early the next day, and baked a cake for the offended teacher before school began.

PASS Monitoring Procedure

Mainstream teachers are responsible for manipulating the monitoring tokens to identify whether student behavior is acceptable, on warning, or in noncompliance. The PASS specialist or paraeducator(s) is responsible for monitoring and recording students' behavior on PASS monitoring forms, removing students when required, and redirecting student behavior. Mainstream teachers are responsible for accepting a student with a clean slate on his or her return to the mainstream classroom.

Here's a typical progression:

- Students begin every class period with an *acceptable* (green color) token showing.

- When a PASS student displays an inappropriate targeted behavior, the mainstream teacher offers the first corrective intervention. ("Jamie, please put down your comic book and return to your math exercise.")

- At this time, the teacher changes the monitoring token from acceptable behavior to the color indicating that the student has been given a *warning* and *behavior needs improvement* (yellow color).

- The student is given a few (1–3) minutes to comply with the teacher's correction. If the student corrects his or her behavior, the teacher changes the token back to the acceptable behavior color. If the student does not change his or her behavior, the teacher changes the token to the *unacceptable* (red color) token to indicate that an *out-of-class intervention is needed*.

- At this point, PASS personnel remove the student from the classroom and redirect the student using a procedure explained later in this chapter.

- After an out-of-classroom redirection by PASS personnel and an appropriate re-entry by the student, the classroom teacher returns the student's monitoring token to the acceptable color.

- If the student refuses to engage in a redirection, indicates an intention to return and engage in the target behavior again, or shows affective instability, the student is escorted to the PASS room for an extended redirection.

Figure 7-2 on the following page illustrates the PASS monitoring procedure.

The monitoring token should be displayed in a location in the mainstream classroom where it can be easily seen by both the student and the PASS monitor in the hallway. At times, a brief communication between the classroom teacher and the PASS monitor may be needed to describe a specific behavior. However, the goal of the PASS Monitoring System is to provide a discreet communication system between the teacher, the student, and PASS staff, thereby reducing the need for discussions that disrupt the classroom routine.

The goal of the PASS Monitoring System is to provide a discreet communication system between the teacher, the student, and PASS staff.

When the PASS monitor observes that a teacher has issued a warning token to a student, the monitor should wait outside the classroom to see if the student self-corrects the inappropriate behavior. If self-correction occurs, the monitor moves on to observe other students but increases the frequency of monitoring for the student who has been on warning.

If the student does not self-correct and misbehavior persists, the monitor gives the student the signal to exit the classroom for redirection.

In instances where the student's behavior has returned to acceptable standards, but the classroom teacher has not had the opportunity to change the token back to the acceptable color, the monitor may unobtrusively change the token to the appropriate color.

Figure 7-2 *PASS Monitoring Procedure*

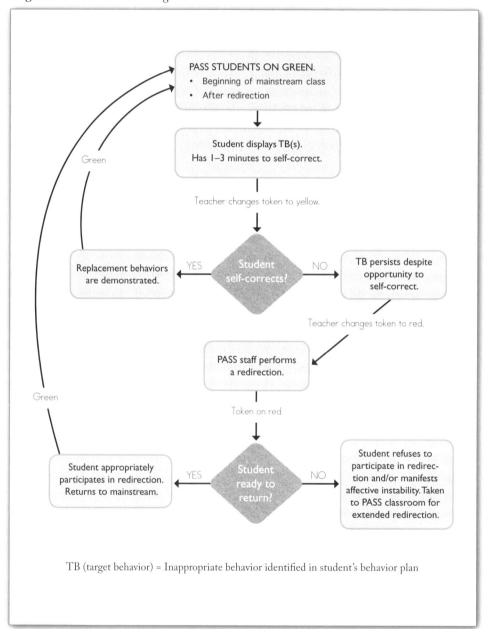

PASS STUDENTS ON GREEN.
• Beginning of mainstream class
• After redirection

Student displays TB(s).
Has 1–3 minutes to self-correct.

Teacher changes token to yellow.

Student self-corrects?

Green

YES — Replacement behaviors are demonstrated.

NO — TB persists despite opportunity to self-correct.

Teacher changes token to red.

PASS staff performs a redirection.

Token on red

Student ready to return?

Green

YES — Student appropriately participates in redirection. Returns to mainstream.

NO — Student refuses to participate in redirection and/or manifests affective instability. Taken to PASS classroom for extended redirection.

TB (target behavior) = Inappropriate behavior identified in student's behavior plan

PASS Monitoring Schedule

Each PASS student is on an individualized monitoring schedule. Initially, PASS personnel monitor students frequently—(every 5 to 15 minutes. As monitoring data indicate that a student is demonstrating appropriate behavior, the schedule is leaned out (e.g., monitoring every 30–60 minutes). Monitoring schedules represent the average length of time between actual monitoring events. The monitor's schedule should not be so predictable that the student can anticipate and adapt his or her behavior accordingly. For example, if a student is on a 15-minute schedule, we do not monitor on the hour and at 15, 30, and 45 minutes after. Rather, we monitor four times in one hour and vary our schedules daily. In addition, if PASS staff observe *PASS Tracker* data that indicates student behavior varies from one setting to the next, PASS might monitor one setting (e.g., Reading) on a 15-minute schedule and another setting (e.g., Physical Education) only once during the hour.

PASS specialists individualize monitoring schedules for each student's developmental needs. For example, younger students may need more frequent monitoring than older ones.

Substitute Teachers and PASS Monitoring

Substitute teachers must be trained in the PASS Monitoring System before they take over the mainstream classroom of a PASS student. Establish policy for office personnel to alert PASS staff whenever a substitute teacher is called to replace a mainstream teacher involved in the program.

PASS personnel should quickly teach substitute teachers how to use the Monitoring System and then increase the frequency of monitoring until the mainstream teacher returns. PASS students should also be told that a substitute will be in their mainstream classroom. PASS staff can encourage appropriate behavior by offering bonus tokens for meeting behavioral goals in the substitute's classroom. We do not recommend removing a student because of a substitute's presence. This situation provides a valuable learning opportunity.

We do not recommend removing a student because of a substitute's presence. This situation provides a valuable learning opportunity.

REDIRECTING INAPPROPRIATE BEHAVIOR

PASS personnel use redirection when a student in a mainstream class has received an unacceptable monitoring token from the classroom teacher for a target behavior. An unacceptable token indicates that the student has already received a warning from the mainstream teacher and has been noncompliant in responding to the teacher's direction and the yellow visual prompt. During redirection, the student tells what happened, identifies what triggered the problem, works on identifying what he or she will do when re-entering the classroom, and finally, describes the consequences of the misbehavior.

PASS personnel follow these basic steps when removing a student from the classroom for redirection:

- The PASS monitor gives a hand signal that indicates the student is to exit the classroom.

- In a private area, the student and PASS specialist engage in the question-and-answer PASS redirection format.

- Once the student demonstrates readiness to return to the classroom, he or she re-enters and engages in appropriate behavior. The mainstream teacher restores the monitoring token to the acceptable color.

Redirection can be accomplished smoothly *only* when the student has participated in training on this procedure during Phase 2: Orientation. During Orientation, the student learns the purpose of redirection (problem-solving) as well as the appropriate exit and re-entry procedures for the mainstream classroom. The student also gains an understanding during Orientation that participating in redirection is not the same as an office referral where a punishment can be expected.

PASS staff repeatedly emphasize to the student that redirection is not a punishment or a disciplinary procedure.

Exiting the Classroom

A PASS monitor uses a hand gesture that means "Come here!" to indicate that the student should exit the mainstream classroom. During Orientation, students learn to exit the class quietly without disturbing other students or instruction. PASS staff repeatedly emphasize to the student that *redirection is not a punishment or a disciplinary procedure.* The function of redirection is to problem-solve and allow the student to return to the classroom with a clean slate.

Case Study

In a bad moment, Tom, a middle school PASS student, begins yelling at his mainstream teacher.

The PASS specialist signals Tom to exit the classroom. Tom and the PASS specialist debrief the incident.

Specialist: *What happened?*

Tom: *She deliberately tried to make me mess up my notebook . . .*

Specialist: *So, how did all this start?*

Tom: *Well, I was working on my art project, and she made me make a mistake and do her old, stinkin' math assignment.*

Specialist: *Can you think how you might have handled this in a way that keeps you out of trouble?*

Tom: *Oh, I guess I could have stopped and done that counting backward thing.*

Specialist: *So, Tom, what are you going to do when you go back into class?*

Tom: *I'll get out her stupid math book and do the stupid work.*

Specialist: *And if you do, what will be the consequence of that?*

Tom: *I get back on green, and I can be Coach's assistant again this week.*

To make restitution, Tom writes a letter of apology and places it on the teacher's desk after school. Later that afternoon, he assists this teacher by carrying several boxes to her car.

Redirecting the Student

Redirection occurs outside the classroom in a private setting. Typically, the location is a hallway close to the student's mainstream classroom and out of sight of other students. However, if the student appears agitated, we often engage in what we call the *walking cure*. That is, we ask the student to walk with us and, while doing so, we observe the student for a de-escalation of agitation. A colleague of ours, Vincent Thomas, developed the practice of asking students to walk with him on his monitoring rounds and always included a trip up or down stairs as a method of facilitating the student's cooldown.

 Avoid inadvertently reinforcing student escape/avoidance behaviors in efforts to calm students. For example, it is not a good idea to have students work out their agitation by engaging in a game of basketball as a deescalation technique.

When an agitated student appears to be able to discuss the situation that resulted in an unacceptable monitoring token, the redirection process begins. We use a verbal technique inspired by the written *Hassle Log* developed by Arnold Goldstein (1988). The verbal prompts we use are:

- *What's going on?* Student relates his or her perception of the problem event. Pay attention to indications that the student perceives hostile attributions for the behaviors of others.

- *What led up to this?* Student identifies triggering events.

- *How could you have handled this differently?* Student identifies T-chart replacement behaviors.

- *What are you going to do when you return to the classroom?* Student indicates intention, or lack thereof, to change behavior.

- *What will be the consequences of that action?* Student demonstrates a cause-and-effect understanding of different behavior choices.

Redirection ends and the student is ready for a return to the mainstream classroom (readiness for re-entry) when he or she:

- Accepts responsibility for the misbehavior

- Relates and/or demonstrates the appropriate replacement behavior

- Exhibits affective control

If the student does not demonstrate these behavioral criteria, he or she does not return to class. Instead, the student proceeds with the PASS monitor to the PASS classroom, where further problem-solving occurs. When the student meets the readiness criteria, he or she returns to the mainstream setting. From the time the student is recorded on red by the monitor until that student returns to the mainstream setting, the monitoring data reflects red and the student earns no credit toward mastery. In addition, parents are informed of the removal to PASS on the School-to-Home note. Serious behavior problems may require that parents be informed by phone, especially if a physical restraint occurs. PASS programs must be aware of campus and state policies regarding the need to inform parents of crisis situations.

RECORDING AND USING PASS DATA

PASS teams analyze behavior using two primary sources of PASS data—PASS Room Logs (Reproducible 7-3) and *PASS Tracker* reports (Figure 7-3).

PASS Room Log

Whenever a student is removed from the mainstream classroom, PASS personnel enter a description of the event in the PASS Room Log. It is important to document a student's removal to the PASS classroom for several reasons. First, removals to PASS should decrease over time. The log data can be used to analyze these trends. In addition, the PASS Room Log provides information that helps identify difficult times of day, problematic classes, and/or teachers with whom a specific student may have difficulty. The student's PASS team may consider this information when making recommendations for alternative interventions or reinforcement. Finally, this data is important documentation for special education funding. Reproducible 7-3 shows a typical PASS Room Log. A blank version is available on the CD.

The PASS Room Log documents:

- The frequency with which a student returns to the PASS classroom

- The purpose for the return

- The setting left by the student

- The length of time the student needs in the PASS classroom before demonstrating readiness to return to the mainstream setting

PASS Room Log

Name	Date	Time In PASS	Reason	Consequences	Time of Return to Class
Carl	10/5	1:30	Review replacement behaviors for leaving class w/o permission	None	2 pm
CJ	10/7	12:45	Verbal aggression toward classmate. Redirection not successful.	One-day ISS. Student apologized to classmate and teacher.	end of day
Sue	10/7	11:15	Refusal to do classwork.	Did makeup assignment.	11:45
Rob	10/9	8 am	Re-Orientation	None	10/14 8 am
Sue	10/14	9:00	Refusal to do homework.	Made up work. Will help teacher collate papers during recess.	11:00

Reproducible 7-3 *PASS Room Log*

PASS Tracker Software

PASS Monitoring Sheets (see Reproducible 7-4a on p. 84) track information used to determine the level of mastery a student has reached on his or her target behaviors. These sheets indicate when the PASS student was monitored in mainstream settings, the appropriateness of the behavior (*acceptable, warning, removal*), and specific identification of any misbehavior the student exhibited.

Information from this form is transferred to the *PASS Tracker* software, which automatically calculates the student's level of mastery. This information is used on a weekly basis to:

- Determine the level of reward for which a student is eligible

- Observe patterns of behavior

- Identify settings that are more problematic than others

- Judge the effectiveness of interventions

PASS Tracker software is an Excel spreadsheet that is provided on the CD.

After staff enters data from PASS Monitoring Sheets into the *PASS Tracker* software, it is available in a report that provides a graphic display of an individual student's behavior over the course of a month. Figure 7-3 shows a sample Behavior Analysis Report, which the student's PASS team can study for frequency of appropriate and inappropriate behavior, the settings where behavior and misbehavior took place, and time of misbehavior. This report also identifies to what extent the student has mastered his or her target replacement behaviors—useful when working with the PASS Reward System.

Furthermore, the Behavior Analysis Report is a tool that helps students see patterns in their own behavior. When this information is shared with students on a regular basis (e.g., weekly), we have seen the form itself function as an incentive for positive behavior.

Students Earn Rewards by:

- Accumulating mastery credit for acceptable behavior in areas identified on behavior plans or documented on monitoring sheets
- Returning School-to-Home notes
- Demonstrating behavior that goes beyond expectations (bonus tokens)

Figure 7-3 *Sample PASS Tracker Behavior Analysis Report*

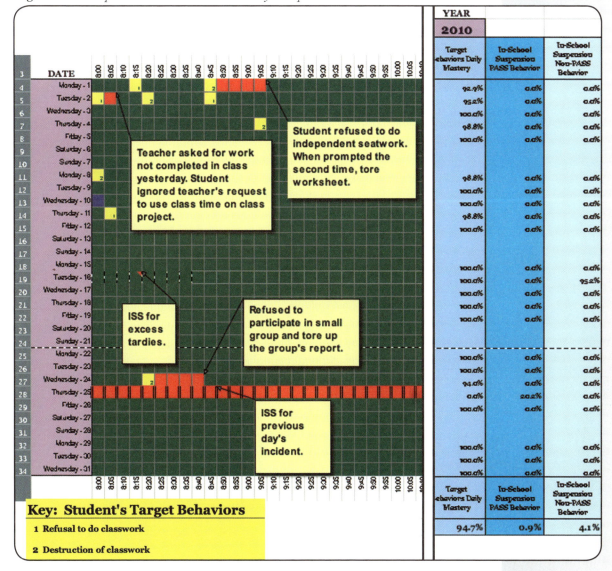

REWARDING APPROPRIATE BEHAVIOR

PASS students receive rewards under two separate circumstances:

- The student demonstrates mastery of targeted replacement behaviors as indicated by monitoring data.

- The student earns a bonus token.

Demonstrating Mastery

PASS employs a two-tiered system of rewards for students who demonstrate mastery of targeted replacement behaviors. Students whose overall mastery of targeted behavior falls within the 60–79% range are eligible at week's end for one category of rewards. Students whose overall mastery of targeted behavior falls within the 80–100% range earn a second category of rewards.

Using data collected on the PASS Monitoring Sheet (Reproducible 7-4a) and input into the *PASS Tracker*, staff determine the percentage level of mastery.

Reproducible 7-4a   *PASS Monitoring Sheet*

Note: There is also a form (Reproducible 7-4b) on the CD with a Friday to Thursday monitoring schedule.

Many programs run their reward system on a Thursday-to-Thursday week. This allows PASS personnel the time to calculate mastery levels for students prior to Friday, when rewards are typically delivered.

When students demonstrate 60–79% mastery of targeted replacement behaviors, they receive lower-level rewards. These rewards are usually a combination of tangible goods such as inexpensive items from a PASS store (e.g., pencils, stickers, combs, notebooks, etc.) and activity passes (e.g., "Get Out of One Math Homework Assignment," 100 on a daily grade, etc.).

Higher-level rewards (80% and above mastery of targeted replacement behavior) generally fall into two types.

Many programs have developed a "Fun Friday" activity. Students are allowed to return to the PASS classroom for a brief period of time during which activities such as board and computer games, short and acceptable films, and food treats are provided.

Though the activities listed above are powerful with some students, particularly younger ones, we recommend the development of reward activities that are available to students only in school settings. For this reason we emphasize the creation of reward activities like meaningful work.

Based loosely on work activities described in the *Administrator's Desk Reference of Behavior Management: Vol. 3* (Sprick et al., 1998), students who achieve 80 to 100% of their behavioral goals are offered assistantships at the end of the reward week. To be effective, these job responsibilities must have high status for the student. For example, Coach's Assistant is a very popular job with PASS students. A student who earns this reward may work with a school coach (volunteer mentor) for about 30 minutes on Fun Friday. To enhance the status of the role, coaches have had shirts and/or badges made with the Coach's Assistant logo, have given whistles to the students to wear around their necks, and have developed jobs such as picking up basketballs from the gym and storing them. The value of this reward increases when coaches use these times to create positive relationships with the students.

Other meaningful work activities that have been effective are Office, Library, Band, and Drama Assistants. The key variables for success are that the student perceives the job as having status and the associated mentor makes an effort to establish rapport with the student. We believe the worth of these activities goes beyond their effectiveness as a reward and supports a student's attachment to school.

Some PASS programs have developed very inventive approaches to differentiating rewards for mastery. In one program with twelve middle school boys, Fun Friday activities included a highly valued basketball game. The length of time that each student was allowed to participate was based upon his percent of mastery of targeted behaviors.

Computing Bonus Tokens

Credit for receiving a bonus token is managed through the *PASS Tracker* software. Anchor on a red cell while simultaneously pressing the Control and B keys. The result is an award of bonus mastery points that is reflected in the mastery percentage of that day. See Appendix A for more details on how to use the *PASS Tracker* software.

PHASE 3
Inclusion & Maintenance

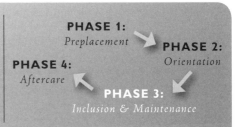

PHASE 1:
Preplacement

PHASE 2:
Orientation

PHASE 4:
Aftercare

PHASE 3:
Inclusion & Maintenance

P hase 3: Inclusion and Maintenance begins after:

1. The PASS student has demonstrated an understanding of:

   • PASS monitoring procedures

   • Replacement behaviors

   • Mainstream class expectations

2. The PASS specialist has determined that the student demonstrates affective control.

The major program activities for Phase 3: Inclusion and Maintenance are:

• Monitoring mainstream settings

• Redirecting inappropriate student behavior

• Correcting behavior

• Managing resistant students and students who are slow to adapt

• Planning for student-initiated classroom removals

• Making decisions for student Re-Orientation

- Planning for beginning and end-of-day activities

- Making adjustments at midyear and holidays

- Planning for self-monitoring

- Making a decision to dismiss a student from PASS

MONITORING MAINSTREAM SETTINGS

Perhaps no other PASS process is as important to the student's behavioral success as monitoring and giving student feedback at the point of performance—the mainstream classroom.

Chapter 7 describes the PASS Monitoring System and how it relates to other PASS processes. It explains:

- PASS monitoring tokens

- Use of bonus token

- PASS monitoring procedure

- PASS monitoring schedule

- Substitute teachers and PASS monitoring

During Phase 2: Orientation, the PASS specialist explains the Monitoring System to students and provides ample time to role-play so that students learn what the four tokens mean and what actions they should take for each one. The specialist also explains how monitoring data is collected and shared.

When the student leaves the PASS room and returns to the mainstream classroom(s) for Phase 3: Inclusion and Maintenance, PASS staff begins monitoring. At this point, the mainstream teacher is responsible for using the monitoring tokens to communicate information about the acceptability of target behavior(s) to the student and to the PASS monitor. PASS personnel are responsible for monitoring the student and recording student behavior on monitoring sheets.

It is important for the mainstream teacher to remember that the monitoring tokens do not reflect the overall behavior of the PASS student in the mainstream setting. They should be used only when the student displays one of the behaviors targeted by the student's behavior plan.

REDIRECTING INAPPROPRIATE STUDENT BEHAVIOR

Redirection is the procedure that PASS personnel use when a student in a mainstream class exhibits one of his or her target behaviors and has been noncompliant in responding to the mainstream teacher's warning and request for appropriate behavior.

Chapter 7 describes the redirection procedure and its use.

In the Orientation classroom, students learn that the redirection process is not a punishment, but rather a method for looking at the problem behavior and devising solutions to prevent its reoccurrence. Student and specialist practice redirection in the PASS classroom until the student understands how to exit the mainstream classroom, how to work through the redirection process, and how to re-enter the mainstream classroom.

When students return to the mainstream classroom in Phase 3, they understand the redirection procedure and how to execute it when their behavior earns an *unacceptable—out-of-class intervention needed* token.

The mainstream teacher is responsible for changing the student's monitoring token back to *acceptable behavior* status when the student re-enters the classroom from redirection. By doing this, the teacher communicates that the student is returning to the classroom with a clean slate.

PASS personnel are responsible for signaling the student to leave the classroom, working with the student through the problem-solving process, judging the readiness of the student to re-enter the classroom, and recording the behavior on the PASS Monitoring Sheet.

Student and specialist practice redirection in the PASS classroom until the student understands how to exit the mainstream classroom.

CORRECTING BEHAVIOR

In Orientation, students learn that there are consequences when target behaviors are not replaced with appropriate behaviors. Those consequences are:

- The student will not earn credit toward mastery and rewards.

- The student will be asked to perform an act of restitution.

While these consequences are explained and practiced in Orientation (see Chapter 6), they are implemented in mainstream settings.

Timing in the delivery of consequences is a critical variable in their effectiveness. When a student misbehaves in the mainstream classroom, does not regain affective control during a redirection, and is escorted by PASS personnel back to the PASS classroom, he or she may be angry. In this case, the student needs time to return to a calm state before anyone can begin instruction in alternative pro-social behaviors or discuss an appropriate act of restitution. We never attempt to deliver a consequence with a student who is in an acting-out state.

Additionally, we never administer consequences without checking the problem situation first, especially if the student insists that he or she was misjudged. It is not uncommon to find that teachers or other students make erroneous assumptions about the guilt of students with emotional or behavioral disorders because of their histories. We find that it is better for all concerned to let students temporarily get away with a target behavior than to punish them for something that they did not do.

MANAGING RESISTANT STUDENTS AND STUDENTS SLOW TO ADAPT

In situations where students appear more resistant to, or more anxious about, placement in mainstream settings, it is helpful to institute the following practices:

- Initially, PASS personnel may stay in the mainstream classroom with the student to make sure that he or she is at ease and that the mainstream teacher demonstrates an understanding of the student's behavior plan.

- Monitor frequently—perhaps every 5 to 20 minutes, if possible.

- If this is an elementary student, give him or her opportunities to participate with the class in nonacademic activities such as recess, movies, and class parties prior to entering more stressful academic settings.

- The specialist should spend as much time as possible observing the student's interactions with other students and the teacher. The specialist can then pass these observations on to the student. Working together, they can problem-solve with role-play activities to resolve problematic issues.

- If the student is not developing positive social relationships, the specialist may need to become an active participant in seeking out students who are positive peer models and who can work collaboratively with the PASS student.

PLANNING FOR STUDENT-INITIATED CLASSROOM REMOVALS

Plans for student-initiated classroom removals should be developed during Phase 2: Orientation. The plan should be developed with the student and communicated to the mainstream teacher.

A student-initiated classroom removal provides an outlet for a student who perceives him- or herself as overwhelmed within the mainstream classroom. The plan for a student-initiated removal provides the student with a strategy for communicating affective distress and getting assistance.

Typically the student initiates removal by signaling the mainstream teacher of the need to return to the PASS classroom. The teacher then changes the monitoring token to red so the PASS monitor can see that there is a problem with the student. The student puts his or her head down on the desk and waits for PASS personnel to effect the removal.

PASS students should always be escorted to the PASS classroom. This ensures that someone is available in the PASS classroom when a student-initiated removal occurs. We also believe that students should not move through unsupervised areas on their way to the PASS classroom because of safety concerns. We view this as an invitation to misbehavior and mishap.

The PASS specialist can use monitoring data and the PASS Room Log to determine whether there is a pattern to events that trigger student-initiated removals. It is also important to determine if the function of the removal is to provide escape or avoidance. With this knowledge, an intervention can be designed to resolve the problem(s).

As with any removal from the mainstream classroom, the PASS student does not receive credit toward mastery during this time.

The plan for a student-initiated removal provides the student with a strategy for communicating affective distress and getting assistance.

MAKING DECISIONS FOR A STUDENT RE-ORIENTATION

"Fall seven times, stand up eight!"

—Japanese proverb

Progression from Phase 2: Orientation through Phase 3: Inclusion and Maintenance is rarely a linear process. Most students experience periodic setbacks in their progress toward fully mainstreamed environments. As a consequence, we think of these two phases as a trial-and-error process with a mix of progress, mistakes, and occasional setbacks. Thus, some students return to the PASS classroom for short periods of time to regroup and receive further instruction and practice on their individualized replacement behaviors. We refer to this step in PASS as Re-Orientation.

Consider Re-Orientation when:

- Students repeatedly display an inability to successfully perform replacement behaviors in a specific setting.

- Students engage in high-level misbehavior that poses a danger to themselves or others.

The decision for a student to return to the PASS classroom for Re-Orientation is data driven. Typically, the student's PASS team meets to review monitoring data and finds that the student is not meeting goals for behavioral mastery. Alternatively, the PASS specialist may make the decision following consultation with program administrators and the student's teacher of record.

Re-Orientation is not a disciplinary action. Consequently, the decision to return a student to the PASS classroom is never made by an administrator or by an individual classroom teacher.

Re-Orientation activities are similar to those performed in Orientation:

- Intensive social skills training in problematic target behaviors

- Structured observations and feedback sessions in the problematic educational setting

- Modified amounts of academic work

The mainstream teacher(s) continue to oversee academic instruction for the student participating in Re-Orientation.

The PASS student transitions back to Phase 3: Inclusion and Maintenance when he or she:

- Successfully performs the pro-social replacement behaviors for the maladaptive behavior that resulted in the decision for the student to participate in Re-Orientation.

- Demonstrates affective control.

If the action that resulted in Re-Orientation involves an injury to another person, the student should be asked to perform restitution. Furthermore, students participating in Re-Orientation are eligible for only lower-level rewards.

The length of time that a student spends in Re-Orientation and the number of classes they spend in the PASS classroom for this activity vary. For example, if the student's target behavior is manifesting in only one classroom during the school day, Re-Orientation occurs only during that period. If misbehavior persists across the school day and in common areas, a full-day Re-Orientation may be more appropriate.

PLANNING FOR BEGINNING AND END-OF-DAY ACTIVITIES

Beginning the Day

Many elementary-level PASS programs have their Phase 3 students begin their day by checking in at the PASS classroom. Students return their School-to-Home notes at this time. In addition, the specialist has an opportunity to assess the student's emotional and behavioral status. If a student displays agitation or distress, he or she may be kept in the PASS classroom, where the student can use replacement behaviors from his or her T-charts in an attempt to de-escalate potentially disruptive escalations of behavior. For example, a student may have been taught self-calming techniques or muscle relaxation practices.

Unless the student exhibits problems at the check-in time, the Beginning the Day routine should be brief.

It is less common at the secondary level for students to begin their day in the PASS room. However, this lack of scheduled contact should be compensated for by having PASS staff start to monitor at the beginning of the first period, with particular focus on watching for affective issues at this time.

Ending the Day

Plans for ending the day must be in place as well. Typically, PASS students are required to report to the PASS classroom late in the school day. At this time, PASS personnel review the daily monitoring sheets with students and give them their School-to-Home notes. This check-in allows the student and specialist to identify successes and problem-solve in preparation for the next school day. If data for the day has been entered into the *PASS Tracker* software, students can also review their mastery of targeted replacement behaviors and their progress toward reward goals.

When end-of-the-day scheduling in the PASS classroom is not feasible, deliver School-to-Home notes to the student's mainstream classroom at the close of the school day. This allows the student to stay in his or her last academic class for the entire period but does not allow for debriefing and problem-solving.

MAKING ADJUSTMENTS AT MIDYEAR AND HOLIDAYS

When PASS students return from prolonged school holidays, there is often a need to intensify PASS services for a brief period. Following long breaks, incorporate an extended beginning-of-the-school-day schedule to review and practice expectations for behavior. Staff may also adjust monitoring schedules to include more frequent rounds in the first few days following a school holiday.

Staff may also adjust monitoring schedules to include more frequent rounds in the first few days following a school holiday.

Another important midyear adjustment is evaluation of student behavior. For example, it may be appropriate to consider moving a student from Inclusion and Maintenance to self-monitoring at midyear.

PLANNING FOR SELF-MONITORING

During Phase 3: Inclusion and Maintenance, PASS staff provides monitoring to support student's efforts to manage their behavior. The ultimate PASS goal is for students to self-monitor their behavior.

As in all program phases, a decision to move students to self-monitoring is driven by data. Self-monitoring is appropriate when an analysis of behavior data from the *PASS Tracker* indicates few unacceptable behavior events.

The PASS team reviews the monitoring forms, *PASS Tracker* data, and PASS Room Logs for the past several months—typically, at least a semester. If the data indicates few behavior problems in targeted areas (i.e., monitoring data reflects mastery at the 90–100% level), and the PASS team concludes that a student appears capable of managing behavior, the specialist schedules a consultation with the student.

The team shares monitoring data with the student to demonstrate the student's readiness for this transition. They assure the student that PASS support will continue and request input from the student before self-monitoring begins. A student's perception of his or her ability to function more independently is a critical variable to success.

Self-monitoring activities typically follow this sequence:

- The student receives a daily Self-Monitoring Form (see Reproducible 8-1) that requires evaluation of target behaviors (usually with 60-minute monitoring intervals).

- The mainstream teacher(s) receive daily monitoring sheets with the same monitoring intervals as those given the student.

- At the end of each school day, data forms are collected from the student and his or her mainstream teachers.

- PASS personnel enter data from the forms into the *PASS Tracker* software.

- The PASS specialist meets with the student on a weekly basis to discuss the data from the mainstream teacher's monitoring sheets and the student's Self-Monitoring Form. The PASS specialist and the student identify variables that contribute to student success and problem solve difficult situations.

PASS Self-Monitoring Sheet

Student __Mary__   Date __5/3__

Note to PASS Students: It is your responsibility to indicate the number of times you demonstrated your target behaviors (TBs) in each class period indicated on this form. Also, indicate with a check mark if you self-corrected that behavior or if PASS personnel had to be called because the behavior continued. At the end of the period, take this form to your teacher. Ask him or her to complete the teacher assessment. On days when a substitute teaches your class, only you need to complete this form. Repeated failure to obtain a teacher's signature may result in a return to PASS facilitated monitoring.

Numbered Target Behaviors are:
1. _Verbal outbursts_
2. _Inappropriate comments to teachers and peers_
3. _____

Student Form:

TB#	Frequency	Self-Correct	PASS Referral	Time/period	Time/period	Time/period	Time/period	Time/period	Time/period	Time/period
1	//	//								
2	///	//	/							

Teacher Form:

TB#	Frequency	Self-Correct	PASS Referral	Time/period	Time/period	Time/period	Time/period	Time/period	Time/period	Time/period
1	//	//								
2	///	//	/							

Student Comments (in weekly review of Self-Monitoring Sheets):
Student believes one comment was just a joke and not inappropriate—teacher got all bent out of shape over nothing. Doesn't see why she should apologize.

PASS Specialist Comments (in weekly review of Self-Monitoring Sheets):
Frequency of verbal outbursts continues to decline. Inappropriate comments are decreasing too. Reviewed what makes a comment inappropriate and how student can behave when someone is offended by what she says. In all, she is doing great!

© 2009 James R. Poole and Hope Caperton-Brown | Reproducible Form

Reproducible 8-1   *PASS Self-Monitoring Sheet*

Making a Decision to Dismiss a Student from PASS

Following a successful period of self-monitoring, a student is considered for dismissal from PASS.

The PASS team makes decisions about recommending dismissal from PASS. Considerations include the length of time the student has been successful and the benefits for the student of graduating from the program. The student can be dismissed from PASS services when he or she has had prolonged success with self-monitoring. Success is typically recognized as an average evaluation from teachers and student of behavioral mastery at the 90–100% level. Usually, this is after a period of at least one semester to one school year. If a student is a participant in special education, a formal IEP meeting is required for dismissal.

Rather than remove PASS support abruptly at this time, PASS staff should take care to celebrate a student's successful transition through the program and make reassurances about the availability of PASS personnel to the student if problems occur.

Invitations to participate in PASS Aftercare provide this reassurance and give the student a sense of enhanced status.

Following a successful period of self-monitoring, a student is considered for dismissal from PASS.

PHASE 4
Aftercare

PHASE 1:
Preplacement → PHASE 2:
Orientation
PHASE 4:
Aftercare ← PHASE 3:
Inclusion & Maintenance

P hase 4: Aftercare begins after:

1. Students have successfully participated in self-monitoring for a significant period of time.

2. The PASS team has determined that there are no more tertiary-level behaviors that require individualized interventions.

3. If the student participates in special education, an IEP team has formally dismissed the student.

We have found that students who successfully complete Phases 1–3 of PASS sometimes revert to their previous misbehavior after exiting from PASS. Typically, these students demonstrate behavioral stability for three to six months without supportive services, but then their behavior begins to decline. To address this issue, we decided to incorporate Phase 4: Aftercare.

Aftercare is designed to provide:

- Support to students who have been dismissed from PASS services

- Peer mentors for students still actively engaged in PASS Phases 1–3

Participation in PASS Aftercare is voluntary. However, PASS graduates are encouraged to participate and serve as PASS sponsors. Sponsorship carries status and builds self-worth while simultaneously reinforcing the maintenance of pro-social behaviors acquired during the student's participation in earlier PASS phases.

Training for PASS sponsors should include lessons in how to listen and how to share their stories. Conceptually, this borrows from the Alcoholics Anonymous model, where individuals with a history of sobriety serve as sponsors to those new to the program.

Training students as sponsors begins with instruction in active listening. For example, potential sponsors are advised to pay close attention to their mentees as they talk about their situations. Sponsors indicate attention by looking directly at the speaker and not engaging in other tasks when the mentee is talking. They can also give physical cues that they are interested in the story they are hearing—nodding occasionally, smiling at appropriate times, saying "yeah" and "uh huh." Finally, after the mentee finishes his or her story, sponsors can summarize the comments they heard and ask questions to clarify points.

PASS graduates are encouraged to participate and serve as PASS sponsors.

Only after the mentee has finished does the sponsor briefly tell his or her own story. The emphasis here is not to glorify or dramatize past misbehaviors. Rather, sponsors are encouraged to talk about the past as a journey—where they were, where they are now, and how they got from there to here.

Aftercare activities typically take place during lunch periods and before or after school. The goal is to have students meet weekly.

The PASS team matches mentor (PASS sponsor) with mentee (PASS student), taking into consideration issues such as similar interests, history, and gender.

PASS personnel supervise all interactions between sponsors and mentees. Though there is no way to impede the relationship outside of the school day, formal mentorship should be in a setting where PASS personnel can oversee the appropriateness of interactions. As always in the PASS program, staff, sponsor, and mentee should all strive for a climate characterized by mutual respect and support.

CHAPTER 10

HANDLING EMERGENCIES

S tudents with emotional/behavioral disorders are in a crisis situation when there is a loss of rationality and the student is judged to be a danger to self and/or others.

During such occasions, first and foremost, PASS personnel should be guided by state laws that govern the management of dangerous and potentially dangerous behavior of students in school settings. *The procedures we suggest here are additional practices for programs to consider and are in no way intended to supplant state mandates.*

Good communication capabilities are essential to the functioning of a PASS program. Communication systems need to be in place when working with students with emotional or behavioral disorders.

Before school starts in the fall, the PASS program specialist and the building principal should meet to decide on the following:

- *Communication device* to be used by PASS personnel to communicate with one another and with front office personnel

- *Crises codes* to use to communicate crisis severity

- *Crisis response training* needed for crisis team members

Communication devices that PASS programs typically use vary from inexpensive walkie-talkies to handheld radios with a number of communication channels. These devices are necessary because immediate communication is required when a student becomes a danger to self or to others. The program specialist and para-educator, as well as the administrator overseeing PASS discipline issues, should all be equipped with this device.

Crisis codes should be predetermined to allow quick communication about the perceived severity of an impending crisis. We suggest three levels of alert:

- Code Green: A crisis may be impending, and the crisis team stands by.

- Code Yellow: An escort is needed. This triggers the crisis team to respond.

- Code Red: Emergency removal of a student and/or assistance with physical restraint is required. The crisis team responds.

All members of the crisis response team should be trained and certified in a recognized crisis response procedure.

Crisis codes should be predetermined to allow quick communication about the perceived severity of an impending crisis.

CHAPTER 11

IMPLEMENTING PASS

I mplementing a PASS program requires a school's commitment to the belief that children and youth with emotional or behavioral disorders can and should be educated with their nonhandicapped peers in the general education curriculum.

Once that philosophical hurdle has been cleared, the next step is to select appropriate staff to facilitate the program, then provide adequate training for those individuals. Successful implementation of PASS requires adequate training for key players.

SELECTING STAFF

Selecting appropriate PASS staff is a crucial component to the success of the PASS program. Typically, PASS operates under the guidance of a PASS specialist with the assistance of a paraeducator. Depending on the number of students admitted to PASS or the intensity of behavior exhibited by students, more paraeducators may be required.

PASS Specialist

The PASS specialist is the focal staff member in PASS implementations. This person is a certified teacher whose assignment is the management of students admitted to the program. The PASS specialist is central to the implementation of PASS and the success of students in the program.

A successful PASS specialist knows the basic principles of behavior management and applies a functional approach to understanding behavior. This staff member employs a positive approach to behavior change and interacts positively and patiently with adults and students. A PASS specialist must be flexible and able to stay calm during crises.

PASS Paraeducator(s)

The paraeducator's role in PASS is critical. PASS programs are always staffed with at least one PASS specialist working in coordination with an assistant.

Like a PASS specialist, a successful PASS paraeducator demonstrates personal maturity, communicates effectively, and has a history of positive interactions with children. He or she is patient and able to maintain calm in crisis.

Figure 10-1   *The PASS Team*

KEY PLAYERS	MUST UNDERSTAND:
Administrators and program supervisors	▪ PASS philosophy and practices
PASS specialist and paraeducator(s)	▪ Different PASS phases ▪ Activities to be completed within each phase ▪ Data collection and data analysis process
Teachers and paraeducators who work with PASS students in mainstream classrooms	▪ Their PASS team roles and duties ▪ All Phase 3 activities that relate to the PASS student
All school staff members	▪ PASS goals ▪ PASS Monitoring System ▪ Staff roles

PROVIDING TRAINING

It is essential that all staff involved with PASS and PASS students receive proper training in their duties and roles. At a minimum, key players must understand the concepts outlined in Figure 10-1.

Prior to the beginning of the school year, the PASS specialist and the school administrator charged with PASS oversight should conduct a brief overview of PASS. This overview should highlight the goals of PASS, the monitoring practices, and the roles of different personnel in the PASS process. The entire school staff should attend this overview. Blackline masters and image files are provided on the CD accompanying this manual should you wish to create a PowerPoint presentation and/or handouts for this staff training. See Appendix B for a list of available materials.

Training the PASS Specialist

The PASS specialist is the key element in PASS. Training for this person is crucial. With the proper understanding of PASS philosophy and practices, this person can adequately train other staff members.

The PASS specialist must understand:

- What the program is and why we need it
- The four-phase process of PASS and all activities associated with each phase
- The roles of each member of the PASS team and how they function together
- The function of the PASS classroom and how to set one up
- How to use the PASS Monitoring and Rewards Systems
- How to conduct redirection procedures
- How to collect and analyze data using a variety of data collection tools and the *PASS Tracker*

Essentially, the PASS specialist must have a thorough understanding of all of the concepts, procedures, and strategies presented in this book.

If you need assistance...

We can assist you with training issues. Visit the PASS website at http://thepassprogram.com for more information and to contact us.

CHAPTER 12

SUPERVISING PASS

The leadership provided by building and district administrative personnel is central to the success of PASS. Leadership begins with support for the philosophy of managing inappropriate student behavior with Positive Behavior Support (PBS) strategies. Administrators are key in creating the understanding that PASS is a behavior education program, not an alternative disciplinary setting. Supervisors also serve to actualize the success of PASS through efforts to maintain the integrity of PASS procedures.

WHO SUPERVISES PASS PROGRAMS?

In most implementations of PASS, administrative personnel at the campus and district level supervise the program.

Typically, a campus principal or assistant principal over-sees the day-to-day running of a PASS program. This administrator manages issues related to campus personnel, student behavior, and parental involvement. On large campuses with multiple administrators, we recommend that one administrator work exclusively with the PASS program and with all PASS students. Assigning only one PASS administrator reduces the

likelihood that personnel will manage students with similar behavior infractions differently. It also ensures that staff follow student behavior plans consistently.

Only one administrator because . . .

Case study

> *Administrators at a large urban high school made the decision for grade-level administrators to manage their own PASS students. On this campus, two cousins in different grade levels were referred to PASS. When they got into a fight with each other, their respective grade-level principals, unfortunately, issued different disciplinary consequences. The mothers of these students, who were sisters, discussed the incident, discovered these discrepancies in disciplinary action, and were justifiably angry. The mainstream teacher in whose classroom the fight occurred was also unhappy with the different approaches to administrative management of the problem. Hence, the recommendation to rely on one administrator for the program.*

In addition to building-level supervision of PASS, a district, particularly a larger one, will assign district-level staff to oversee the integrity with which PASS practices are implemented across the district. In our experience, this role has been assigned to various individuals—district behavior specialists, school psychologists, at-risk coordinators, and special education administrators.

TRAINING OF PASS SUPERVISORS

It is particularly helpful for a PASS supervisor to have experience with assessing behavior using a Functional Behavior Analysis (FBA) approach.

Regardless of their role within a district, individuals selected to supervise PASS must demonstrate a thorough understanding of PASS philosophy, PASS practices, and the roles of the PASS specialist and the mainstream teachers who work with PASS students. In addition, it is particularly helpful for a PASS supervisor to have experience with assessing behavior using a Functional Behavior Analysis (FBA) approach. Experienced PASS specialists often serve well as district-level PASS supervisors.

We strongly recommend that program supervisors have the training and experience described above for two reasons.

First, without such training and experience, the potential exists to create a program that does not adhere to the PASS philosophy or rely on best practices.

> *This occurred in a large middle school. No campus administrator had an understanding of PASS. The management of the program was left with a*

specialist who misrepresented PASS practices to the administrator. Parents of a student complained about PASS, specifically punitive disciplinary techniques used by the PASS specialist. The administrator was unable to respond to parent queries about program practices. Upon further inquiry, the PASS specialist was unable to provide documentation from PASS training or the PASS manual to support the punitive approach to behavior management that had been instituted.

Second, when program supervisors thoroughly understand PASS, they are more capable of hiring appropriate PASS personnel. When Jim Poole was employed as a teacher in his first behavior program, the hiring administrator took a look at him and said, "You're a big guy—you can handle this group." The implication in this statement was that an imposing physical presence was the defining characteristic of his employment and that the supervisor perceived the management of crises as the central responsibility of this job. In contrast, experience has shown that, regardless of size, individuals who are successful PASS specialists have skill sets that include:

- Reliance on behavior management using a Positive Behavior Support approach

- Communication skills and an ability to relate to adults as well as students

- An understanding of an FBA approach to analyzing behavior

- Comfort with crisis management

- Patience and optimism

Supervising PASS Activities

In general, supervisors of PASS programs will observe:

- PASS staff as they engage in activities to facilitate the program (Orientation, Reorientation, Monitoring, reinforcement of behavior mastery, and PASS team meetings)

- Documentation associated with PASS

Supervisors may wish to use a checklist such as Reproducible 12-1 to guide their observations.

Reproducible 12-1 *PASS Administrator's Checklist*

PASS Adminstrator's Checklist

REPRODUCIBLE
12-1

Orientation:

✓ 1. PASS specialist manages student behavior in PASS classroom through direct instruction in expectations for behavior. (That is, students are given rules for when it is appropriate to talk with others, how they ask for help, how expectations differ for different activities, when movement around the room is acceptable, and the teacher's expectations for student participation in different classroom activities [using the CHAMPs model].)

_____ 2. PASS specialist provides instruction in PASS Monitoring System and reward system. *See notes on back.*

✓ 3. PASS specialist instructs and models replacement behaviors identified on student's behavior plan.

✓ 4. PASS specialist provides role-play opportunities for students in replacement behaviors identified in student's behavior plan.

✓ 5. PASS specialist escorts student to mainstream classroom for structured observation and student feedback experience.

_____ 6. PASS specialist facilitates student completion of a modified amount of academic assignments from teacher of record. *See notes on back.*

Reorientation:

✓ 1. PASS specialist provides instruction in replacement behavior(s) identified on student's behavior plan, focusing on those that precipitated the Re-Orientation.

✓ 2. PASS specialist escorts student to mainstream classroom where problem behavior occurred for a structured observation and student feedback experience.

✓ 3. PASS specialist facilitates student completion of a modified number of academic assignments from teacher of record.

Monitoring:

✓ 1. PASS specialist consistently monitors students (or supervises the monitoring by PASS paraeducators) and uses PASS monitoring sheets to document student behavior.

✓ 2. When monitoring indicates that a student's behavior is unacceptable, PASS staff provide a PASS redirection.

✓ 3. Target behaviors that result in a removal for redirection are analyzed using the PASS FBA Worksheet.

Reinforcement:

_____ 1. PASS specialist has developed a two-tiered system of reinforcement that is contingency based and delivered on (at least) a weekly basis. *See notes on back.*

PASS Team Meetings:

✓ 1. PASS specialist schedules PASS team meetings on a regular basis, sends invitations to meetings to team members, creates a meeting agenda, and provides updated behavior analysis information from PASS Tracker.

Documentation:

✓ 1. Portfolios have been developed for each student and delivered to all of the student's mainstream teachers and campus administration. Portfolios contain student profile, student schedule, IEP/behavior plan, suggested behavior management strategies appropriate for mainstream classroom application, student t-charts, and student work samples.

✓ 2. Monitoring sheets are maintained for all students. Self-monitoring sheets are provided to students who have achieved acceptable mastery of target behaviors.

✓ 3. Data from monitoring sheets are entered into PASS Tracker on a timely (weekly) basis.

_____ 4. Behavior Analysis reports are developed for each student and are used for intervention planning, delivery of reinforcement, and PASS team consideration. *See notes on back.*

✓ 5. PASS Room Logs are maintained and include information about all student returns to PASS classroom from mainstream settings.

✓ 6. A record of school-to-home communication and/or parent contact is dutifully kept.

Observing PASS Orientation

Orientation is the second PASS phase. All students new to the PASS program *must* participate in this phase. When observing the PASS classroom, supervisors should expect to see new students recently identified as candidates. However, there may be times during the year when there are no students in the PASS classroom.

It is possible that all of the students are participating in Phase 3: Inclusion and Maintenance—thus, the empty room.

Because Orientation occurs within the self-contained PASS classroom, we expect the PASS specialist to create a setting that elicits and supports appropriate behavior and facilitates the speedy behavior education that we emphasize in this program phase. We recommend that specialists use the CHAMPS model (Sprick, 2009; Sprick, Garrison, & Howard, 1998). In this model, the classroom is organized and managed in such a way that behavior expectations are taught, practiced, and implemented for each classroom activity. Supervisors who observe chaotic Orientations may need to provide support to the PASS specialist in this area.

The focus during Orientation is education about PASS expectations and practices and behavior education in the specific area(s) targeted by the student's behavior plan. Therefore, supervisors should expect to see the PASS specialist provide instruction in the PASS Monitoring and Reward Systems. In addition, a substantial amount of the school day should be devoted to instruction in replacement behaviors for the target behavior(s) identified on the student's behavior plan.

PASS behavior education follows a cognitive-behavioral model, wherein the PASS specialist first explains the replacement behavior, then models the behavior, provides opportunities for role-play by the student, and provides repeated practice opportunities.

Before any student exits Orientation and begins the next phase of inclusion in mainstream classes, supervisors should expect that the specialist and the student have observed at least one or two of the mainstream classrooms in which the student will participate—a Classroom Observation and Student Feedback experience.

Finally, program supervisors should expect to observe PASS students engaged in a reduced amount of academic work that is provided by the teacher of record, not by the PASS specialist.

Observing Re-Orientation

Re-Orientation is a Phase 3 activity that occurs in the PASS classroom. It transpires after the PASS team observes monitoring data and identifies a need for more intensive behavior education in one or all of the target behaviors identified on the student's behavior plan. As is true of Orientation activities, it is possible that when a supervisor observes PASS, no students are participating in this activity.

The focus during Orientation is education about PASS expectations and practices and behavior education in the specific area(s) targeted by the student's behavior plan.

When a Re-Orientation is taking place in the PASS classroom, supervisors should expect to observe the PASS specialist providing instruction (using the previously described cognitive-behavior model) in replacement behaviors for the target behaviors that have resulted in a PASS team recommendation for a Re-Orientation. This may include reworking the student's T-chart or practicing replacement behaviors previously taught in Orientation. Before any student returns to a mainstream class from Re-Orientation, supervisors should expect that the PASS specialist and the student have observed the setting where the target behavior occurred and have mutually engaged in problem-solving a way to be successful in this setting in the future. The Classroom Observation and Student Feedback Form (see Reproducible 6-2 in Chapter 6) facilitates this process.

As with Orientation, there may be a minimal amount of academic work completed by the student during this activity. The focus and majority of student time is spent on behavior education. The goal is to teach the replacement behavior and facilitate a quick turnaround for the student's re-engagement in mainstream classes with instruction from subject-area and grade-level teachers.

Observing PASS Monitoring

PASS monitoring staff are often among the most visible personnel on a school campus, and this should be the expectation of PASS administrators. When supervisors observe PASS monitoring, they should see PASS staff carrying a clipboard with monitoring sheet, T-chart, and PASS FBA worksheet for each student. These various forms facilitate data collection on any target behavior that has received a red monitoring token from the mainstream teacher. In addition, campus administrators should expect to see monitoring tokens in all mainstream classes where PASS students are placed. These tokens should be in clear view of the student for whom they are intended and visible to the PASS staff from the classroom door. At times, teachers are slow to change token colors. Administrators can accelerate this process by reminding teachers that the tokens are intended to reflect the current status of a target behavior. As such, they communicate behavioral expectations to students without the need for continued verbal reminders from the teachers.

If a PASS staff member is observed removing a student from a mainstream classroom for a redirection, then supervisors should expect the staff member to use the five PASS redirection prompts:

- What's going on here?

- What led up to this?

- How could you have handled this differently using your replacement behaviors?

- What are you going to do when you return to the classroom?

- What will be the consequences of that action?

Consistency across PASS staff in the manner in which they redirect is a program goal. Consequently, the PASS specialist and the PASS paraeducator should handle redirection in the prescribed manner and in such a way to reinforce behavior education.

Observing Reinforcement

PASS supervisors should observe a two-tier reinforcement system. In the PASS model, lower levels of behavior mastery are rewarded differently than higher levels of mastery. PASS specialists are expected to create such a system using both token reinforcers and activity reinforcers. This system should be in place prior to the start of the school year. There is no expectation in PASS that students will demonstrate appropriate replacement behavior *because they should*.

Observing PASS Team Meetings

It is the responsibility of the PASS specialist to schedule frequent PASS team meetings. This involves organizing the meeting—sending invitations to PASS team members and creating a meeting agenda. All PASS team meetings should be problem-solving in nature. We expect that the specialist will facilitate this agenda by presenting data from the *PASS Tracker* so that members of the PASS team can observe behavior using an FBA approach. PASS administrators support these expectations with their regular attendance at these meetings.

All PASS team meetings should be problem-solving in nature.

Supervising PASS Documentation

The PASS process is data driven, and consequently, the PASS supervisor must monitor a variety of data collection measurement tools.

Student Portfolio

By the time a student completes Orientation, PASS supervisors can expect to see a Student Portfolio for that student. These portfolios should be provided to all mainstream teachers who educate this student. The PASS administrator should also receive a copy of the portfolio.

PASS Monitoring Data

PASS supervisors should expect to be able to review at any time PASS Monitoring Sheets that reflect the status of the target behaviors at the time of the monitoring observation. On the back of the monitoring sheet, supervisors should expect to see completed T-charts for each of the student's target behaviors.

On a weekly basis, program supervisors can expect to see that monitoring data has been entered into the *PASS Tracker* software to actualize behavior analysis. It is the practice in many districts for *PASS Tracker* data and PASS Behavior Analysis Reports to be e-mailed to program supervisors on a weekly or monthly schedule.

PASS Room Log

Supervisors of PASS should ask to see the PASS Room Log to review whether it is accurate and current. The Room Log enables the PASS team to assess the amount of time that a student spends in the PASS classroom as opposed to the mainstream classroom. This data has several important purposes. For instance, if the student is in special education, a coding system to track his or her participation in mainstream is a requirement. The PASS Log also indicates the frequency with which the student returns to the PASS room. This allows the PASS team to determine whether escape or avoidance is the function of the misbehavior that resulted in a removal.

School-to-Home Communications

Finally, we view parents and guardians of PASS students as partners in the PASS process. Records of School-to-Home notes and other forms of parent contact are important to document the progress of this partnership and should be available to supervisors for review.

It is expected that PASS will be well understood by all campus staff.

SUPERVISION ISSUES RELATED TO EFFECTIVE COMMUNICATION

It is expected that PASS will be well understood by all campus staff. Ensuring that this is the case is an important responsibility for the PASS specialist and a critical area for supervisory oversight.

As mentioned in the previous chapter, it is crucial for campus staff to understand the key elements of the PASS process and practices. The PASS administrator, together with the PASS specialist, should present an overview of PASS to all staff prior to the start of the school year. Participation by the principal communicates to staff that there is administrative support for the philosophy and practices inherent in the program.

Supervisory presence at PASS team meetings is vital. Teacher participation in these meetings directly correlates with the regular attendance of a campus administrator. In addition, building supervisors are often effective at maintaining a problem-solving focus during these brief, but frequent, reviews of student progress.

Many PASS programs have established weekly meetings of the PASS specialist, building administrator, and district PASS supervisor. In these meetings, the PASS specialist shares information about personnel, student crises, and parental issues. This regular communication ensures that supervisors will stay aware of critical program and student issues.

POTENTIAL HOT SPOTS FOR SUPERVISOR AWARENESS

Additional issues that may appear on PASS campuses and are best managed by program supervisors include:

- Misusing PASS monitoring tokens

- Using substitute teachers

- Misusing the PASS classroom

Misusing PASS Monitoring Tokens

Occasionally, mainstream teachers may misuse PASS monitoring tokens, especially in the early implementation of the program. Typically, this means that the teacher uses the tokens in a generic fashion, changing the token color for any and all misbehavior displayed by the student. Teachers should read the Student Portfolio for PASS students in their classes. The Student Portfolio includes a T-chart that identifies the specific target behavior (TB) for that student and the replacement behaviors the student has been taught during behavior education in the PASS classroom. Teachers should change PASS monitoring tokens *only* when the student displays a TB. If a problem arises in a teacher's use of tokens and the PASS specialist is unable to change this behavior by educating the teacher about token use, the building administrator's assistance may be needed.

Using Substitute Teachers

Substitutes in any classroom often elicit misbehavior on the part of students. To address this issue, campus administrators may establish a routine for the front office to inform the PASS specialist of the presence of a substitute. The PASS response will be to increase the frequency of monitoring and provide extra incentives to students who manage their behavior under these more taxing situations.

If the PASS specialist or paraeducator is absent, campuses often find that a familiar staff member who has a previous relationship with the PASS student and who is trained in PASS makes a better substitute than a stranger. Thus, it works better when the familiar staff member stands in for the missing PASS specialist or paraeducator and the substitute takes over for the staff member.

Misusing the PASS Classroom

Mainstream teachers sometimes engage in the dangerous practice of sending the PASS student back to the PASS classroom as a consequence for misbehavior or to complete missing work.

If the student is acting out, he or she should not be sent to a room where there may be no staff present (PASS staff are very likely to be monitoring classrooms if there are no students in Orientation or Re-Orientation). Students return to PASS only when accompanied by a PASS staff member and only when their participation in a redirection has not been successful.

If teachers wish to send students to the PASS room to complete missing classwork, they need to be reminded that PASS is not content mastery—it is a behavior education setting. Furthermore, when PASS staff must engage in academic assistance, they cannot fully fulfill their behavior monitoring and behavior education duties. Establishing this role clarification is an administrative issue.

Glossary of Terms

Amends. Making amends compensates someone for a loss or injury. In PASS, making amends is part of the restitution process that a student experiences when he or she hurts or injures someone else by displaying a targeted behavior. In making amends, we strive to find an action that relates in some way to the behavior. So, if a student destroys another student's notebook, for instance, an appropriate act of amends would be for that student to purchase a replacement notebook and give it to the other student. Making amends helps to repair the damage to the relationship between the student and the victim, teaches the student that there are consequences to his or her actions, and helps the student achieve self-management of his or her behavior.

Behavior Improvement Plan (BIP). A BIP is a set of strategies and timelines designed to help students with emotional or behavioral disorders learn acceptable pro-social behaviors to replace the maladaptive behaviors they currently use. Federal law requires that a BIP be developed for those students identified under Individuals with Disabilities Education Act (IDEA) guidelines as "seriously emotionally disturbed." In this book, we often refer to a *behavior plan*. For students with a disability, this behavior plan is a BIP.

Direct Instruction. Developed by Siegfried "Zig" Engelmann and introduced in the 1960s, Direct Instruction (DI) is a teaching method that has been highly successful in accelerating the learning of at-risk students. In a DI approach, teachers provide explicit instruction and define tasks clearly, present concepts by breaking them down into smaller sub-skills, offer ample opportunity to practice to mastery, and offer positive descriptive feedback and immediate corrective feedback. In PASS, the specialist uses DI to teach students PASS expectations and activities by providing a clear explanation of expectations, teacher demonstration and modeling, ample time for interactive practice and role-play, corrective feedback, and positive descriptive feedback of the expected behavior.

Emotionally/Behaviorally Disturbed (EBD, SED, ED, BD, etc.). These acronyms are among those used to describe students with emotional, behavioral, or mental disorders. Under the Individuals with Disabilities Education Act (IDEA), students with these issues are categorized as having a *serious emotional disturbance*, which the law further defines as "a condition exhibiting one or more of the following characteristics over a long period of time and to a marked degree that adversely affects educational performance—

1. An inability to learn that cannot be explained by intellectual, sensory, or health factors;

2. An inability to build or maintain satisfactory interpersonal relationships with peers and teachers;

3. Inappropriate types of behavior or feelings under normal circumstances;

4. A general pervasive mood of unhappiness or depression; or

5. A tendency to develop physical symptoms or fears associated with personal or school problems." [Code of Federal Regulations, Title 34, Section 300.7(b)(9)]

In this book, we use EBD to refer to students who qualify under IDEA for special education services. However, it is important to note that not all students with emotional or behavioral issues fall under the above definitions. Consequently, in this book we use the more inclusive "emotional or behavioral" phrase to refer to both special and general education students.

Functional Behavior Assessment (FBA). An FBA is a tool that can identify the reason a student engages in a particular behavior (i.e., the function the behavior serves for the student). Usually conducted by a highly skilled interventionist (e.g., school psychologist), a formal FBA commonly involves structured interviews, teacher rating scales, questionnaires, and direct observation in a natural environment. Using these techniques, the interventionist tries to determine the antecedents (what precedes the behavior) and consequences (what follows the behavior) of the behavior under analysis. In PASS, we use an FBA worksheet to gather antecedent and consequence data when a student displays a target behavior. In addition, schools may require a formal FBA conducted by the school psychologist during Preplacement as a prerequisite for placement in PASS.

Levels System. Levels systems (a.k.a., point and levels systems) are behavior management tools commonly used with students who display challenging behaviors. These systems have been in use for many years; however, recent research indicates that they are not that effective in bringing about lasting behavior change. Nonetheless, many schools still rely on some form of a levels system in their self-contained classrooms.

Levels systems operate on points earned for appropriate behavior that then translate to a level of reward. For instance, students in the self-contained classroom can earn a point every time they follow directions the first time they are given or stay on task and complete assignments on time. At the end of the counting period (often a week), students may trade their point cards in for rewards, which are given out according to the number of points (or a percentage of compliance) the student has earned. For example, if a student earns 150 points or more, he or she can select from Level One rewards, 100–149 points, Level Two rewards, and so on.

There are problems with levels systems in that they frequently rely on a set of points and levels that apply to the entire class. Hence, they do not address individual behavior concerns. In addition, research seems to indicate that they do not help students make lasting changes in their maladaptive behaviors.

Other Health Impaired (OHI). *Other health impaired* refers to students with "limited strength, vitality, or alertness due to chronic or acute health problems that adversely affect educational performance." Students with OHI fall under federal definitions for special education services.

Point of Performance. *The point of performance* refers to the point in time and space when and where appropriate behavior is commonly manifested. For PASS students, the point of performance is the mainstream classroom at any point during the school day.

Positive Behavior Support (PBS). According to the U.S. Department of Education, PBS is "a general term that refers to the culturally appropriate application of positive behavioral interventions and systems to achieve socially important behavior change." PBS involves the use of interventions that focus on explicitly teaching expectations for academic and behavioral success, treating students with dignity and respect, and working collaboratively with staff, parents, and community to foster student behavioral change. PASS endorses and incorporates the PBS approach.

Readiness. When we use the term *readiness* in PASS, we are describing the student's level of preparedness to:

1) leave Orientation and enter the mainstream classroom and

2) re-enter the mainstream classroom after redirection.

In the first case, the student is ready to enter the mainstream classroom when:

- The student demonstrates appropriate replacement behaviors as alternatives to the maladaptive behaviors targeted on the behavior plan.
- The student understands the monitoring and rewards systems.
- The student understands behavioral expectations for entering and leaving mainstream classrooms.
- The student exhibits affective control.

After redirection, the student is ready to return to the mainstream classroom when:

- The student accepts responsibility for the misbehavior.
- The student relates and/or demonstrates the appropriate replacement behavior.
- The student exhibits affective control.

Redirection. Redirection is the PASS procedure used when a student in a mainstream class exhibits one of his or her target behaviors and does not comply with the mainstream teacher's warning and request for replacement behaviors.

Redirection occurs after the student is removed from the classroom and regains control of his or her emotions. PASS personnel ask the student a series of questions designed to help the student discuss what happened, why it happened, how it could have been prevented, and what happens now. When the student displays readiness for re-entry to the mainstream classroom, redirection ends.

Replacement Behaviors. Replacement behaviors are appropriate, pro-social, positive behaviors identified on a student's behavioral plan. These behaviors are meant to replace the target behaviors that impede the student's educational progress. These are the behaviors that PASS staff explicitly teach, and they are unique to each individual student.

Restitution. In PASS, restitution involves two actions: an apology followed by an act of amends. Restitution carries the message, "If you broke it, you fix it." It fosters student awareness and responsibility and opens up an opportunity for student self-evaluation. As a result, many PASS consequences involve a restitution of some type.

Target Behaviors. Target behaviors are the maladaptive behaviors that prevent students from achieving academic and behavioral success in school. They are identified in each student's behavior plan along with their respective replacement behaviors.

Appendix A

PASS Tracker Manual

TABLE OF CONTENTS

INTRODUCTION

The *PASS Tracker* is a Microsoft Excel spreadsheet that operates on both Windows and Macintosh computer systems. Every day, the PASS specialist or paraeducator enters data taken from PASS Monitoring Sheets (Reproducible 7-4a or 7-4b) into the *Tracker*. Embedded macros then calculate daily and monthly mastery levels, which PASS staff can use to determine individual reward levels for PASS students.

ORGANIZATION

This manual is divided into two sections. "Section 1: Working with Excel" describes how to use Excel to perform specific tasks that you need to know how to do before you can enter student data into the *Tracker*. You will learn:
- How to use control keys
- How to open contextual menus
- How to select cells
- How to work with comments

These are fairly basic tasks, so if you have worked with Excel before, you can skip "Section 1: Working with Excel" and go directly to "Section 2: Working with *PASS Tracker*," starting on p. 124.

"Section 2: Working with *PASS Tracker*" describes how to use the *PASS Tracker* to record data about student behavior and generate reports. You will learn:
- How to install the *PASS Tracker* on your computer
- How to initialize the *PASS Tracker* template to reflect your school year and calendar
- How to work with each individual student *Tracker*, from creating the student file to printing a weekly report

CONVENTIONS

Throughout this manual, we will use these conventions to represent keystrokes and key names:
- When we want you to use a key combination (that is, press two keys at the same time), we capitalize key names and combine them with a plus sign, as in CTRL+C.
- When we refer to a command that you execute from a menu, we first identify the menu by name and follow it with the greater than symbol (>) and then the command, as in File>Save As.
- When we refer to a particular key, we capitalize its name, as in ENTER.
- On some keyboards, you use the RETURN key to enter data. On other keyboards it's the ENTER key. In this manual, we use the term ENTER to refer to both keys.
- If you are using a Macintosh desktop computer, you probably do not have a CTRL key. Instead, use either the APPLE key or the CONTROL key in key combinations.

....
  WARNING: Do NOT move cells on the *PASS Tracker* spreadsheet. Doing so may prevent
  the formulas and macros from functioning correctly.
....

SECTION 1: WORKING WITH EXCEL

Our purpose in this section is to provide instruction on the basic Excel skills you need to use the *PASS Tracker*. We are assuming that you have used computers before, can use the mouse to navigate, and have a basic understanding of how to work with files.

Excel is a Microsoft product that enables a user to open a workbook (i.e., Excel file) that consists of several worksheets. A worksheet (or spreadsheet) is made up of cells arranged in columns and rows in which the user enters data. Excel uses embedded formulas to allow the user to manipulate this data.

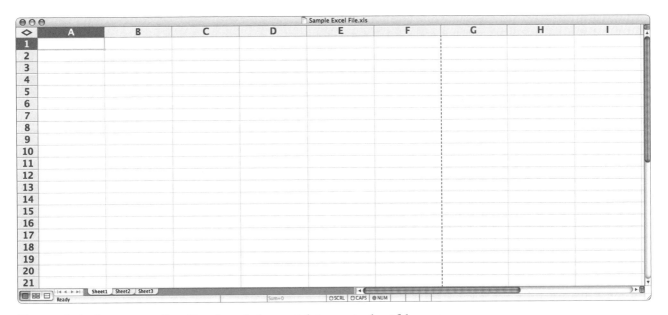

Figure A-1: A portion of an Excel worksheet with its typical grid layout

At the bottom of Figure A-1 are three tabs: Sheet1, Sheet2, and Sheet3. These are three separate worksheets, all of which are contained in the workbook called Sample Excel File.xls. The workbook name is identified at the top of the window in the Excel title bar.

Excel is a complex program that allows a user to do a lot with data, but to use the *PASS Tracker* you need to know very little—most notably how to select cells and how to use comments. But first we need to describe how to use handy keystrokes that make data entry faster and easier.

USING THE CTRL KEY

Holding the CTRL key down while simultaneously pressing other keys enables you to perform a variety of tasks. These are the CTRL key combinations you will frequently use in *PASS Tracker*:

CTRL+C   Copy the contents of a cell
CTRL+V   Paste the contents of a cell
CTRL+R   Record a PASS noncompliant (redirection) behavior
CTRL+K   Record a PASS behavior in In-School Suspension
CTRL+L   Record a non-PASS behavior in In-School Suspension
CTRL+B   Record a bonus token
CTRL+I   Mark an information cell
CTRL+G   Restore cell to default value

USING CONTEXTUAL MENUS

A contextual menu displays a list of commands relevant to a particular item. For instance, you can display a contextual menu that contains commands related to columns, as shown in Figure A-2.

To display a contextual menu, do one of the following:

> Press the CTRL key and simultaneously click on the item.

> OR

> If you have a two-button mouse, right-click on the item.

In this text, we use the first method, only because not everyone has a two-button mouse. If you do, feel free to use the second method.

Figure A-2: Contextual menu for columns

SELECTING CELLS

To select a single cell, click on it. Excel marks selected cells by highlighting the border, as illustrated in Figure A-3.

To select a range of cells, click on the first one and drag across the cells in the range. Release the button when you've included all the cells you want to select. Notice that the border is highlighted.

Figure A-3: Selected cell B2

WORKING WITH COMMENTS

You can attach a comment to any cell in the worksheet. Comments allow you to record descriptions and other pertinent facts about student behavior.

To add a comment:

1. Hold CTRL down and click the cell to which you want to add the comment. This displays the contextual menu.
2. Select Insert Comment from the contextual menu. This opens the comment box.
3. Type your comment text in the box.
4. When you finish typing the text, click anywhere outside the comment box. This closes the comment box and places a small red triangle in the upper right corner of the cell.

To delete a comment:

1. Hold CTRL down and click the cell that contains the comment you want to delete.
2. Select Delete Comment from the contextual menu.

To display comments, do one of the following:

> To display all of the comments on the worksheet, open the View menu at the top of the screen and click Comments.

> OR

> To display an individual comment, hold CTRL down and click the cell that contains the comment. Then select Show Comment from the contextual menu.

To resize or move comments:

Resize a comment box by using the sizing handles (those square boxes at each corner and along the sides). Position your cursor over a sizing handle and drag to resize.

Move a comment by grabbing any border of the box away from the sizing handles and dragging.

> NOTE: You can move or resize a comment box when you create it. If you want to move or resize a comment box after you've closed it, you must first display it.

SECTION 2: WORKING WITH PASS TRACKER

The *PASS Tracker* is located on the CD that accompanies this book. Look for a file named *PASS Tracker.xlt*.

INSTALLING PASS TRACKER

To install the *PASS Tracker* application, you need the following minimum requirements:

	Windows	Macintosh
Processor	Intel Pentium 223 MHz or faster processor (Pentium III recommended)	G3, Mac OS X-compatible processor or higher
Operating system	Microsoft Windows 2000 with Service Pack 3 (SP3), Windows XP, or later	Mac OS X version 10.2.8 or later
Memory	128 megabytes (MB) of RAM or more	256 MB of RAM
Hard disk	150 MB of available hard disk space; optional installation files cache (recommended) requires an additional 200 MB of available hard-disk space	450 MB for a recommended installation, 630 MB for a full drag-and-drop installation
Drive	CD-ROM or DVD drive	CD-ROM drive (or connection to a local area network if installing over a network)
Display	Super VGA (800 x 600) or higher resolution	1024 x 768 or higher resolution displaying thousands of colors
Software	Excel 2003 or 2007	Excel 2004 or 2008 for Mac

To download the *PASS Tracker* from the CD:

1. Put the CD in your CD drive.
2. Double-click on the PASS Toolkit CD icon to open an Explorer (Windows) or Finder (Mac) window.
3. Drag the file PASS Tracker.xlt onto your desktop. You may store this file anywhere on your computer or leave it on your desktop for convenient access.
4. Double-click on the file icon to open the *PASS Tracker* template. When the system prompts you to enable or disable macros, indicate that you want to enable them.

> NOTE: You will need to enable macros whenever you open a *PASS Tracker* file.

PASS Tracker Screen

Before we describe how to use the program, take a moment to familiarize yourself with the *PASS Tracker* interface, shown in Figure A-4.

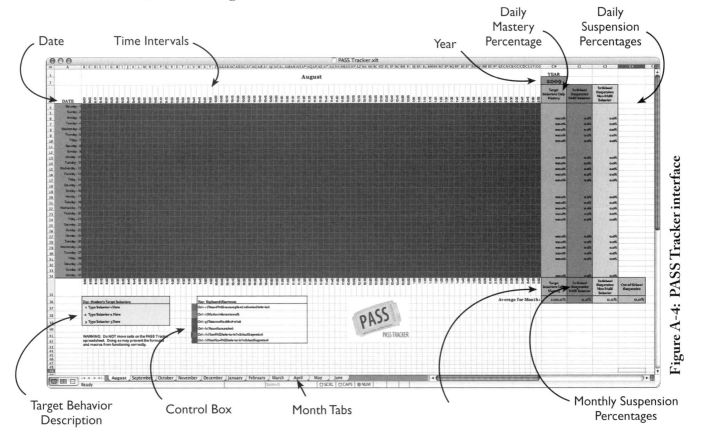

Figure A-4: PASS Tracker interface

The name of the file appears in the title bar at the top of the window. When you first open it, it should say *PASS Tracker.xlt*. The extension "xlt" means that this file is an Excel template. It is the pattern you will use to create each individual student file. You'll learn how to do that later in this appendix.

The template contains a data tracking page for each month of the school year, beginning in August and ending in June. You see these as tabs in the bar at the bottom of the window. Click on any tab to open the worksheet for that month.

The large green area in the center is where you enter data about student behavior. Notice that it is a simple grid divided into days and dates along the vertical axis and five-minute time increments along the horizontal axis.

You use the yellow block below the data entry grid to enter the student's target behaviors. The block to the right of that is a legend or key for the controls you use to record data on student behavior.

Immediately to the right of the data entry grid is the year, which you will change at the beginning of each school year. Changing the year in this box will automatically reconfigure days and dates for the month.

To the right of the year box are three columns of percentage data. These reflect:
- Calculations for the student's daily mastery of his or her target behaviors
- The percentage of time a student displays a PASS targeted behavior in an in-school suspension
- The percentage of time a student displays a non-PASS misbehavior in an in-school suspension

Note that weekends, while listed in the Date column on the far left, are not listed in these columns.

The final four boxes at bottom right contain monthly percentages for target behavior mastery and both in-school and out-of-school suspensions.

Now that you've studied its screen, let's look at what you will need to do to use *PASS Tracker*:
- Tailor the *PASS Tracker* template for your school year.
- Create student *PASS Tracker* files.
- Enter student data collected on daily PASS Monitoring Sheets.
- Produce reports to share with the student, the student's parents, and the student's PASS team.

Tailoring the PASS Tracker Template

The *PASS Tracker* is designed to adapt to individual school calendars as well as schedules for individual students. The following sections detail how to add or delete months as well as accommodate school holidays.

> WARNING: When you work on the template file, keep in mind that any changes you make will be propagated to every copy of the template that you create (e.g., a new student file). Also, any copy of the template created before the modification will not be updated with the new information. Consequently, we strongly recommended that at the beginning of the school year, you enter all school holidays into the template and tailor your school year before you create any student files.

Deleting Months

Some schools begin their years in August and end in May; others start school in September and end in June. To accommodate these different schedules, the *PASS Tracker* begins in August and ends in June (see Figure A-5).

> WARNING: Do NOT move cells on the *PASS Tracker* spreadsheet. Doing so may prevent the formulas and macros from functioning correctly.

You can delete extraneous months by following these steps:

1. Press CTRL and click on the name of the month that you want to delete in the tab bar at the bottom of the window.
2. On the contextual menu, select Delete. The *PASS Tracker* warns you that the sheet will be permanently deleted and asks you to select OK (to delete) or Cancel (to cancel the deletion).
3. Click OK to delete the worksheet for that month.

Figure A-5: Delete any months you don't need

Modifying the Year

The *PASS Tracker* is designed to automatically update the Date column each year. But you need to tell it to do so (see Figure A-6).

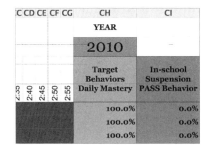

1. Open the worksheet for the first month of your school year (August or September).
2. In the Year column, select the year cell.
3. Type in the current year and press ENTER. Notice that the days and dates in the Date column change to match the calendar.

Figure A-6: Year column

4. Repeat this procedure for each month of your school year. (Remember, the year changes in January!)

Modifying the Dates of a School Year

The *PASS Tracker* automatically excludes weekends from its calculations of daily and monthly mastery. However, it can't know when your school is not in session because of grading or staff development days. Nor does it track federal, state, and local holidays. You will also have to tell it when school is closed for winter and spring breaks. In the *PASS Tracker*, you mark all of these days as holidays (see Figure A-7).

To add a holiday:

1. Click on the day in the Date Column on the left. This highlights the border of that cell.
2. Type the word "Holiday" and press ENTER. Note that the Daily Mastery percentage for that day disappears.

Figure A-7: All days when school is not in session must be marked as holidays

To mark a series of days as a holiday (e.g., spring break):

1. Mark the first day of the series as a "Holiday," just as you did above.
1. Click on the newly added holiday cell. This highlights the borders of the cell.
2. Position your cursor over the lower right corner of the cell. Your cursor will change from a white plus sign to a black plus sign.
3. With your cursor in that position, hold your mouse button down and drag along the Date column to the ending day of the series.
4. When the highlighted box encloses the end day, release your mouse button. This fills the selected cells with the word "Holiday" and erases the Daily Mastery percentages for all of the days you modified.

To restore a holiday (in case you mark the wrong day):

1. Click on a day that is not marked "Holiday." This highlights the cell border.
2. Press CTRL+C to copy the selected cell. A moving border appears around the highlighted box, indicating that it is ready to be pasted.
3. Click on the day you want to restore.
4. Press CTRL+V to restore the date. Note that the Daily Mastery percentage reappears.

Saving Your Changes

Use CTRL+S to save the changes you've just made to the template. These changes will appear in any student file you create from this moment forward.

CREATING STUDENT FILES

Now that you've set up your template (*PASS Tracker.xlt*), you can create files for each of your students.

1. If the *PASS Tracker* template is closed, double-click the *PASS Tracker.xlt* icon or name. When prompted, indicate that you want to enable macros.
2. When the *Tracker* opens, select File>Save As.
3. In the Save As box, type in the student's name —e.g., "John Doe.xls." Note: the file extension for this file is "xls." It is a spreadsheet, not a template.

Notice that you are now editing the new student file, as indicated by the file name in the title bar at the top of the screen. The template has been closed.

To create a second student file, reopen the template (*PASS Tracker.xlt*) and start with Step 2 above. You will need to repeat this for as many students as you have.

Entering Student Data

The *PASS Tracker* keeps track of a student's absences, misbehaviors, target behaviors, and suspensions. You may also record notes about the student's behavior in the *Tracker*.

Modifying Behavior Descriptions

The first thing you may want to do is record the target behaviors for the student (see Figure A-8). Do this in the yellow box below the green data entry grid.

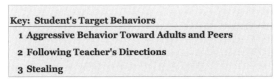

Key: Student's Target Behaviors

1	**Aggressive Behavior Toward Adults and Peers**
2	**Following Teacher's Directions**
3	**Stealing**

Figure A-8: Sample target behaviors

PASS Tracker can track up to three target behaviors for a student. To add or modify descriptions of these behaviors:

1. Click on the cell to the right of one of the numbers in the yellow box.
2. Type the description of the behavior and press ENTER.

Recording an Absence

Recording student absences is done in the same way as adding a holiday, except instead of "Holiday," use the word "Absent," as follows:

To record a single day a student is absent:

1. Click on date the student is absent in the Date column on the left.
2. Type the word "Absent" and press ENTER. Note that the Daily Mastery percentage for that day disappears.

To mark a series of days that a student is absent:

1. Mark the first day of the series as "Absent," as you did above.
2. Click on the newly added "Absent" cell.
3. Position your cursor over the lower right corner of the cell.
4. With your cursor in that position, hold your mouse button down and drag along the Date column to the ending day of the series.
5. Release the mouse button. This fills the selected cells with the word "Absent" and erases the Daily Mastery percentages for the days you've modified.

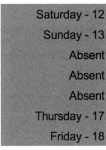

Saturday - 12
Sunday - 13
Absent
Absent
Absent
Thursday - 17
Friday - 18

Figure A-9: Indicate days when the student is absent

To restore a day you've marked as absent:

1. Click on a day that is not marked "Absent."
2. Press CTRL+C to copy the selected cell.
3. Click on the day you want to restore.
4. Press CTRL+V to restore the date. Note that the Daily Mastery percentage reappears.

Recording a Target Behavior

Record this data whenever a student displays a target behavior but responds appropriately after a teacher correction (monitoring token on yellow).

Target behaviors are listed in the yellow box at the bottom of the page. They are numbered from one to three.

To record that a student displayed a target behavior:

1. Select the cell that represents the date and the time that student displayed the behavior.
2. Type the number that corresponds to the displayed behavior and press ENTER.

> NOTE: Behaviors cannot be noted on weekends or school holidays. Behaviors are noted in individual five-minute increments.

Recording Noncompliant Behavior

Record this data whenever a student displays a target behavior, does not respond to teacher correction, and is removed from the classroom for a redirection (monitoring token on red).

To record that a student did not comply with the mainstream teacher's warning and was removed for redirection (see Figure A-10):

1. Select the cells that reflect the time during which the behavior occurred.
2. Press CTRL+R to modify the selected cells. They will change to red, and the Daily and Monthly Mastery boxes will update automatically.

Figure A-10: Example record of noncompliant behavior

> WARNING: Do NOT move cells on the *PASS Tracker* spreadsheet. Doing so may prevent the formulas and macros from functioning correctly.

To add information about the misbehavior:

1. Hold CTRL and select any modified red cell to display the contextual menu.
2. Select Insert Comment from the contextual menu.
3. Record the information in the comment box.

NOTE: Noncompliant behavior cannot be noted on weekends or school holidays and can be added only to a single day at a time.

Recording a PASS Behavior in In-School Suspension

Record this data when a student displays a PASS target behavior while in an in-school suspension.

To indicate a PASS behavior during an in-school suspension:

1. Select the cells that reflect the time during which the behavior occurred.
2. Press CTRL+K to mark the time period as a suspension. Double lines appear at the beginning and at the end of the time period. Behaviors noted within these double lines are reflected as a percentage in the In-school Suspension PASS Behavior column to the right. These cells also turn red, and the Daily and Monthly Mastery percentages change.

To remove the suspension:
1. Select all of the cells.
2. Press CTRL+K to remove the double lines and restore the percentages in the In-School Suspension PASS Behavior column to their default values.
3. Press CTRL+G to restore the cells to the default values and green color.

Recording a Non-PASS Behavior in In-School Suspension

Record this data when a student displays a non-PASS target behavior while in an in-school suspension.

1. Select the cells that reflect the time during which the behavior occurred.
2. Press CTRL+L to mark the time period as a suspension. Dashed lines appear at the beginning and at the end of the time period. Behaviors noted within these dashed lines are reflected as a percentage in the In-school Suspension Non-PASS Behavior column to the right.

To remove the suspension:

1. Select all of the cells.
2. Press CTRL+L to remove the dashed lines and restore the percentages in the In-School Suspension Non-PASS Behavior column to their default values.

Recording an Out-of-School Suspension

To record an out-of-school suspension:

1. Click on date for which the student is out on suspension.
2. Type the word "Suspension" and press ENTER. Note that the Daily Mastery percentage disappears for that day and that the Out-of-School Suspension Monthly Average box is updated.

To mark a series of days that a student is out on suspension:

1. Mark the first day of the series as a "Suspension," as you did above.
2. Click on the newly modified cell.
3. Position your cursor over the lower right corner of the cell.
4. With your cursor in that position, hold your mouse button down and drag along the Date column to the ending day of the series.
5. Release the mouse button. This fills the selected cells with the word, "Suspension," erases the Daily Mastery percentages for the days you've modified, and updates the Out-of-School Suspension Monthly Average.

To restore a day you've marked as a suspension:

1. Select a day that is not marked as "Suspension."
2. Press CTRL+C to copy the selected cell.
3. Click on the day you want to restore.
4. Press CTRL+V to restore the date. Note that the Out-of-School Suspension Monthly Average is also updated.

Recording a Bonus Token

Record this data when a student receives a blue PASS monitoring token for behavior above and beyond the replacement behaviors identified on his or her behavior plan.

When a student earns a bonus token by performing an act of restitution or other agreed-on behavior, the student receives credit toward mastery in the *PASS Tracker*.

To record a bonus:

1. Select a red cell that marks the misbehavior for which the student is making amends.
2. Press CTRL+B. The red cell changes to blue and the Daily and Monthly Mastery percentages increase.

Marking Informational Cells

To add informational cells:

1. Select the cell or cells you want to mark as informational.
2. Press CRTL+I to change the cell color to gray. Neither the Daily nor the Monthly Mastery box is affected.
3. Hold CTRL and click on a gray cell to display a contextual menu
4. Select Insert Comment from the contextual menu to open a comment box.
5. Record the information.

> NOTE: Informational cells cannot be noted on weekends or school holidays and can be added only to a single day at a time.

Restoring Cells to Default Values

To restore cells to their defaults:

1. Select the cell or cells you want to restore.
2. Press CRTL+G. The system will prompt for confirmation.
3. To proceed with the restore, select Yes. The cells change to green, and the Daily and Monthly Mastery boxes update automatically.

> NOTE: Cells can be restored only a single day at a time.

PRODUCING STUDENT REPORTS

Using the *PASS Tracker*, you can print a Student Behavior Analysis Report that you can share with the student and the student's PASS team. This report is essentially a screen shot of a student's monthly *PASS Tracker* worksheet.

Before you print, you need to set up a few things. You may want to display all comments (see p. 123 in Section 1 for more information about comments), and you will need to format the report.

Formatting the PASS Tracker Report

Excel provides a variety of ways for you to format your document so that it prints exactly the way you want. You can set paper options to specify document size, layout, and orientation. You can use page breaks to control where content continues to the next page and add headers, footers, and report titles.

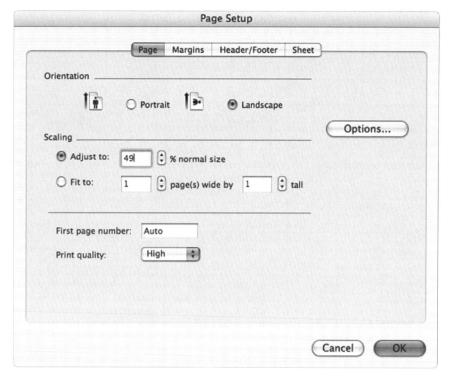

You can do most of what you want to do with a report in Page Setup.

Select File>Page Setup to open the Page Setup box shown in Figure A-11.

Figure A-11: Page Setup options in Excel

By selecting a button at the top of the Page Setup window, you can:

- Adjust page orientation and scaling (Page)
- Adjust page margins (Margins)
- Assign headers and footers (Header/Footer)
- Set the printer order of pages (Sheet)

Using Page Setup, you can add the student's name as a title to the report, add a date or page number to a footer, set your page orientation to portrait or landscape, and define margins. We won't tell you exactly what to do, but rather invite you to experiment with the settings in Page Setup.

If you want to preview your report, select File>Print Preview to open the Print Preview window. You can open the Page Setup window from there by selecting the Setup button.

Print Preview and Page Setup provide you with all of the tools you need to tailor your report.

TROUBLESHOOTING

The *PASS Tracker* software will display error messages when you try to do something that is not allowed—for example, assign a suspension on a weekend day. On the following pages are some questions that may come up when using the *PASS Tracker*.

➤ **<u>I can't save individual student information. What's the problem?</u>**

You are trying to save to a read-only disk. Instead, copy the *PASS Tracker* spreadsheet to your hard drive and then enter individual student data.

➤ **<u>My macros aren't working. What do I do?</u>**

Macros won't work if macros aren't enabled in Excel. With some versions of Excel, you will be prompted to enable macros when you open the *PASS Tracker* file. Select the button to Enable Macros. In other versions, the spreadsheet will open but macros are disabled because of Excel's security settings. Check the area above the spreadsheet for a security warning. If macros are disabled, select the option to enable them.

Note: Support for macros was removed in Excel 2008 (Macintosh only), so the PASS Tracker spreadsheet will not work in that version of the software.

Moving spreadsheet cells will break the links that allow the macros and formulas to function properly. If your CTRL+key combinations stop working, check to see if any cells have moved (compare your spreadsheet to the template file). Moving the cell back to its original location may fix the macro problem. If that doesn't work, you will need to return to the spreadsheet template and create a new spreadsheet.

➤ **<u>How do I set up a new school calendar each year?</u>**

PASS Tracker has a perpetual calendar. Just change the number in the year cell, as desired

➤ **<u>It's a leap year, but the February sheet has only 28 days. How can I add the extra day?</u>**

First, make sure the year cell is set to the leap year. *PASS Tracker* won't let you add an extra day if the year is not a leap year. The date cell will display this string instead: #value!.

On the February sheet, add a new row at the bottom of the grid. Do this by selecting the last row in the grid, right-clicking, and selecting Insert from the contextual menu. Copy one of the working date fields and paste into the new date field to display the proper date for the added day.

➤ **<u>What happens if we have school during the month of July?</u>**

Add a new sheet by copying one of the existing sheets with 31 days (Edit>Move or Copy Sheet). Click on the bottom tab to rename the sheet.

➤ **What do I do if student is suspended, in clinic, in principal's office, or absent?**

Review the legend at bottom of the spreadsheet for instructions, or consult the manual. If student is absent, write "absent" in the column for school date.

➤ **The Daily Mastery calculations aren't updating. What do I do?**

The spreadsheet contains built-in formulas that perform automatic calculations such as the Daily Mastery percentage. The spreadsheet will not work properly if these formulas are changed. Find a *PASS Tracker* page that is working properly (another month, or generate a new file from the *PASS Tracker* template), and copy and paste the affected cells from the good sheet to the broken one. If that doesn't fix the problem, you will need to return to the spreadsheet template and create a new spreadsheet.

➤ **The Daily Mastery calculation is less than 100% even though no target behaviors appear for that day.**

Daily Mastery calculations will be inaccurate if you enter an incorrect number (anything other than the 1, 2, and 3 that designate the target behaviors). The incorrect number will not change the grid color to yellow, but it will be counted as a target behavior incident in the Daily Mastery calculations. The default value for a green cell is 5. If you have a row that you think may contain a wrong number, you can select all cells in that row and use CTRL+G to restore the default value. Alternatively, you can step through the cells in the row and watch for the renegade value in the function field at the top of the spreadsheet. When you find it, use CTRL+G to restore that cell.

➤ **I entered an ISS for a PASS behavior by mistake, and CTRL-G won't restore the default cell values. What should I do?**

CTRL+K works differently from the other key combinations used to record PASS data. To remove an In-School Suspension for a PASS behavior, select the affected cells and press CTRL+K again. This will remove the double lines and restore the default values for the percentages in the In-School Suspension Non-PASS Behavior column. The press CTRL+G to restore the cells to their default values and green color.

➤ **I entered an ISS for a non-PASS behavior by mistake, and CTRL-G won't restore the default cell values. What should I do?**

CTRL+L works differently from the other key combinations used to record PASS data. To remove an In-School Suspension for a non-PASS behavior, select the affected cells and press CTRL+L again. This will remove the dashed lines and restore the default values for the percentages in the In-School Suspension Non-PASS Behavior column.

➤ <u>**Can I change the font size of the comments?**</u>

You can change the appearance of the cells in the *PASS Tracker*. You can change cell colors, grid lines, and the fonts and font sizes used in comments. Do not change the location of cells or try to calculate percentages manually.

➤ <u>**Why can't I open the *PASS Tracker* from the CD?**</u>

If you aren't able to open the *PASS Tracker* from the CD, make sure your computer meets the minimum system requirements outlined on p. 124.

➤ <u>**When I double-click the *PASS Tracker* file on the CD, I get this message: There is no default application specified to open the document "PASS Tracker.xlt." What should I do?**</u>

Select the Choose Application button and navigate to your copy of Microsoft Excel. You could also try copying the *PASS Tracker.xlt* file to your computer before double-clicking on it.

➤ <u>**Can I save *PASS Tracker* spreadsheets as xlsx files?**</u>

PASS Tracker uses the .xls (Excel spreadsheet) and .xlt (Excel template) file formats, which are the default file formats in versions of Excel prior to Excel 2007. Excel 2007 (Windows) introduced the .xlsx and .xlst formats, which are not compatible with previous versions of Excel. If you use Excel 2007 or 2008 and have no need to open these files on older versions, you can save the *PASS Tracker* spreadsheets in .xlsx format. However, if you anticipate any need for compatibility with older versions, be sure to save in .xls format.

➤ <u>**I've followed the suggestions here, and still have problems. What should I do next?**</u>

If your problem persists, open the *PASS Tracker* template file (from the CD, if needed) and save a new spreadsheet. Copy your data from the old sheet to the new one (use Paste Special and select values only so you don't inadvertently copy any bad formulas).

➤ <u>**I copied all my data to a new *PASS Tracker* spreadsheet, but still no luck.**</u>

If you are unable to resolve the problem, call Pacific Northwest Publishing at 1-866-542-1490 or e-mail support@pacificnwpublish.com for further assistance.

➤ <u>**My comments aren't printing. What can I do?**</u>

Open the Sheet tab in the Page Setup window. If you want to print comments as you see them on your screen, select As Displayed on Sheet from the drop-down menu in the Comments field.

➤ I receive the following error message when I try to open the PASS Tracker in Microsoft Excel 2008 on a Macintosh computer:

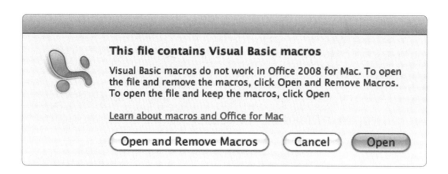

The PASS Tracker software is an Excel spreadsheet with embedded VBA (Visual Basic for Applications) macros that automate the calculations once you enter raw data from your observation sheets. Microsoft removed VBA support from Excel 2008, a Macintosh-only version that was released in January 2008. That means the **PASS Tracker will not run on Excel 2008**. To find out what version of Excel you are using, open the program and select About Excel from the Excel menu.

Excel 2011, released in October 2010, restored support for VBA.

Appendix B

Contents of the CD

1_REPRODUCIBLE FORMS

PASS Repro 3-1   The PASS Program: Positive Approach to Student Success
PASS Repro 6-1   School-to-Home Note
PASS Repro 6-2   Classroom Observation & Student Feedback Form
PASS Repro 7-1   PASS FBA Worksheet
PASS Repro 7-2   How to Use Monitoring Tokens
PASS Repro 7-3   PASS Room Log
PASS Repro 7-4a PASS Monitoring Sheet (Monday–Friday monitoring schedule)
PASS Repro 7-4b PASS Monitoring Sheet (Friday–Thursday monitoring schedule)
PASS Repro 8-1   PASS Self-Monitoring Sheet
PASS Repro 12-1 PASS Administrator's Checklist
T-Chart Template

2_BLACKLINE MASTERS FOR TRAINING

Blackline Master 1: PASS—Positive Approach to Student Success (This can also be used in conjunction with or instead of PASS Repro 3-1 to introduce the PASS program to parents.)
Blackline Master 2: Working with a PASS Student in Your Classroom (This can also be used in conjunction with PASS Repro 7-2 when working with mainstream classroom teachers.)
Intervention Pyramid (PDF of Figure 5-1)
Interrelationship of PASS Orientation Components (PDF of Figure 7-1)
PASS Monitoring Procedure (PDF of Figure 7-2)
The PASS Process
Token Guide (PDF of the colored token figure)

3_SAMPLES

Behavior Analysis Report (Sample)
Sample Student Portfolio
Sample T-charts

4_PASS TRACKER

PASS Tracker Software
PASS Tracker Manual

References and Valuable Resources

Arnold, M. E., & Hughes, J. N. (1999). First do no harm: Adverse effects of grouping deviant youth for skills training. *Journal of School Psychology, 37,* 99–115.

Bandura, A., Ross, D., & Ross, S. (1961). Transmission of aggression through imitation of aggressive models. *Journal of Abnormal and Social Psychology, 63,* 575–583.

Bandura, A., Ross, D., & Ross, S. (1963). Imitation of film-mediated aggressive models. *Journal of Abnormal and Social Psychology, 66,* 3–11.

Barkley, R. A. (1998). *Attention-Deficit Hyperactivity Disorder: A handbook for diagnosis and treatment* (2nd ed.). New York: Guilford.

Bradley, R., Henderson, K., & Monfore, D. A. (2004). A national perspective on children with emotional disorders. *Behavioral Disorders, 29,* 211–223.

Clark, H. B., & Heinemann, M. (1999). Comparing the wraparound process to positive behavior support: What can we learn? *Journal of Positive Behavior Interventions, 1,* 183–186.

Committee for Children (2002). *Second step: A violence prevention curriculum.* Seattle: Committee for Children.

Crone, D. A., & Horner, R. H. (2003). *Building positive behavior support systems: Functional behavioral assessment.* New York: Guilford.

Dishion, T. J., & Andrews, D. W. (1995). Preventing escalation in problem behaviors with high-risk young adolescents: Immediate and one-year outcomes. *Journal of Consulting and Clinical Psychology, 63,* 001–011.

Dishion, T. J., & Kavanagh, K. (2003). *Intervening with adolescent problem behavior: A family-centered approach.* New York: Guilford.

Dishion, T. J., McCord, J., & Poulin, F. (1999). When interventions harm: Peer groups and problem behavior. *American Psychologist, 54,* 755–764.

DuPaul, G. J., & Eckert, T. L. (1997). The effects of school-based interventions for ADHD: A meta-analysis. *School Psychology Review, 26*, 5–27.

Father Flanagan's Boys' Home (1989). *Working with aggressive youth: A sourcebook for child-care providers.* Boys Town, NE: Boys' Town Press.

Fister, S. L., & Kemp, K. A. (2009). *Teach all, reach all: Instructional design and delivery with TGIF.* Eugene, OR: Pacific Northwest Publishing.

Goldstein, A. P. (1988). *The prepare curriculum: Teaching pro-social competencies.* Champaign, IL: Research Press.

Gossen, D.C. (1998). *Restitution: Restructuring school discipline.* Chapel Hill: New View Publications.

Harrower, J. K. (1999). Educational inclusion of children with severe disabilities. *Journal of Positive Behavior Interventions, 1*, 215–230.

Horner, R. H., & Carr, E. G. (1997). Behavioral support for students with severe disabilities: Functional assessment and comprehensive intervention. *Journal of Special Education, 31*(1), 84–104.

Horner, R. H., Dunlap, G., Koegel, R. L., Carr, E. G., Sailor, W., Anderson, J. A., et al. (1990). Toward a technology of "nonaversive" behavioral support. *Journal of the Association for Persons with Severe Handicaps, 15*, 125–32.

Individuals with Disabilities Act of 1997, 20 U.S.C. 1415 et seq.

Jenson, W. R., Rhode, G., & Reavis, H. K. (2010). *The tough kid tool box.* Eugene, OR: Pacific Northwest Publishing.

Kasani, J. H., Jones, M. R., Bumby, K. M., & Thomas, L. A. (1999). Youth violence: Psychosocial risk factors, treatment, prevention, and recommendations. *Journal of Emotional and Behavioral Disorders, 7*, 200–210.

Larson, J. (2005). *Think first: Addressing aggressive behavior in secondary schools.* New York: Guilford.

Larson, J., & Lochman, J. E. (2002). *Helping school children cope with anger.* New York: Guilford.

Lavelle, L. (1998). *Practical charts for managing behavior.* Austin, TX: Pro-Ed.

Maag, J. W. (2005). Social skills training for youth with emotional and behavioral disorders and learning disabilities: Problems, conclusions, and suggestions. *Exceptionality, 13*(3) 155–172.

Meichenbaum, D. (2001). *Treatment of individuals with anger-control problems and aggressive behaviors: A clinical handbook*. Clearwater, FL: Institute Press.

No Child Left Behind (2001). Retrieved March 18, 2005, from www/ed/gov/nclb/overview/intro/index.html.

Parker, H.C. (1992). *The ADD hyperactivity handbook for schools: Effective strategies for identifying and teaching students with Attention Deficit Disorders in elementary and secondary schools*. Plantation, FL: Impact Publications.

Quinn, K. P., & McDougal, J. L. (1998). A mile wide and a mile deep: Comprehensive interventions for children and youth with emotional and behavioral disorders and their families. *School Psychology Review, 27*, 191–203.

Reavis, H. K., Sweeten, M. T., Jenson, W. R., Morgan, D. P., Andrews, D. J., & Fister, S. L. (1996). *Best practices: Behavioral and educational strategies for teachers*. Longmont, CO: Sopris West.

Rhode, G., Jenson, W. R., & Reavis, H. K. (1992). *The tough kid book*. Longmont, CO: Sopris West. Note: Second edition available in 2010 from Pacific Northwest Publishing.

Scheuermann, B., Webber, J., Partin, M., & Knies, W.C. (1994). Level systems and the law: Are they compatible? *Behavior Disorders, 19*, 205–220.

Schneider, B. H., & Leroux, J. (1994). Educational environments for the pupil with behavior disorders: A "best evidence" synthesis. *Behavior Disorders, 19*, 192–204.

Sprick, R. S. (2009). *CHAMPS: A proactive and positive approach to classroom management* (2nd ed.). Eugene, OR: Pacific Northwest Publishing.

Sprick, R. S., Garrison, M., & Howard, L. M. (1998). *CHAMPS: A proactive and positive approach to classroom management*. Longmont, CO: Sopris West.

Sprick, R. S., & Howard, L. (1995). *The teacher's encyclopedia of behavior management: 100 Problems/500 Plans*. Eugene, OR: Pacific Northwest Publishing.

Sprick, R. S., Wise, B. J., Marcum, K., Haykin, M., Howard, L. M., & Garrison, M. (1998). *Administrator's desk reference of behavior management*. Eugene, OR: Pacific Northwest Publishing.

Topper, K., Williams, W., Leo, K., Hamilton, R., & Fox, T. (1994). *A positive approach to understanding and addressing challenging behaviors*. Burlington, VT: Center for Developmental Disabilities, The University Affiliated Program of Vermont.

U.S. Department of Education (2001). Retrieved February 6, 2009, from www.ed.gov/about/reports/annual/osep/2001/index.html.

Wagner, M. M. (1995). Outcomes for youths with serious emotional disturbance in secondary school and early adulthood. *Future of Children, 5*, 90–112.

Walker, H.M. (1995–1997). *The acting-out child: Coping with classroom disruption* (2nd ed.). Longmont, CO: Sopris West.

Walker, H. M., & Walker, J. E. (1991). *Coping with noncompliance in the classroom*. Austin, TX: Pro-Ed.